DOCTRINE
VS.
TRUTH

DARRYL GEE

ISBN 978-1-0980-4394-0 (hardcover)
ISBN 978-1-0980-4395-7 (digital)

Christian Faith Publishing, Inc.
832 Park Avenue
Meadville, PA 16335
www.christianfaithpublishing.com

Printed in the United States of America

Contents

Preface

This is a book given by the inspiration of God to dispel many of the *doctrines* that have been set forth that do not follow God's *truths*.

One of the writers of Proverbs stated, "with all thy getting get understanding" (Prov. 4:7). For whatever reasons, many sermons, passages in books, plays, movies, etc., have "Thus sayeth the Lord" written on them. A lot of this has been done without a clear understanding of what God was really saying or doing! Now we know God's word says He "is not the author of confusion" (1 Cor. 14:33). The scripture also tells us "that no prophecy of the scripture is of any private interpretation" (2 Pet. 1:20). Now I have stated these passages only to convey that God **never** intended for His word to cause confusion within the body of Christ or that any one individual would claim to have the interpretation no one else has. Nevertheless, while Solomon scribed a truth, "there is no new thing under the sun" (Eccl. 1:9), sometimes hidden truths are revealed in time. Paul once scribed, "Now to him that is of power to stablish you according to my gospel, and the preaching of Jesus Christ, according to the revelation of *the mystery, which was kept secret since the world began*, But now is made manifest, and by the scriptures of the prophets, according to the commandment of the everlasting God, made known to all nations for the obedience of faith" (Rom. 16:25–26, emphasis added). Paul also scribed, "How that by revelation he made known unto me the mystery; (as I wrote afore in few words, Whereby, when ye read, ye may understand my knowledge in the mystery of Christ)" (Eph. 3:3–4). God reveals things in His time.

My prayer is that every person who reads and researches the scriptural information given in this book would approach it with no preconceived notions of what this writing may or may not be about. Simply allow God to open your understanding. Do not read this with information you've heard in past sermons. My prayer also is that you would allow God to develop the skill in you to rightly divide His word so that you might fully see what He is saying. This is not to say no one can understand, but that those who lack understanding would be enlightened more. A well-renowned author and minister once said that a good teacher is one who can still be taught and a great leader is one who can still follow. My father in the faith once stated we must learn to eat the meat and throw the bones out. Therefore, keep the meat of that which you consider substance and discard that which you consider not profitable. Finally, remember that while there may be many applications of God's word, there is only *one* interpretation of it in any given scripture. Keep in mind an application is how you apply God's word in any given situation. Where an interpretation is exactly what God meant! There are many doctrines of man versus truths of the Bible, but we'll only touch on a few this time.

You will notice many references to pastors in this work, not to criticize them. These references are only to bring notice to their responsibility of accountability for the health of their flock. We all have a level of accountability for our purpose in this walk. Some have more than others. That doesn't place one above the other, but it only brings notice to our places and purpose.

Acknowledgments

I first want to thank the Lord for selecting me to pen a few truths needed for His bride.

I next want to thank my wife, Mia, for being patient with me as I took much of the time I could have been spending with her to nurture our relationship. However, she recognized that God had a bigger purpose that would actually be considered short. Thank you, baby.

I would like to thank my mother Janet and father George who put me in a place to establish a foundation of faith. A special thanks to my mother for being an example of one who remains steadfast in ministry no matter the storms that arise.

I would like to thank my father in the faith, Pastor Lafayette, for displaying what a real man of God looks and sounds likes when he spends time in God's word.

A final word of thanks to my current pastor, Pastor West, for allowing me to take time out of the music ministry in order to complete this work God has given me.

"Therefore, my beloved brethren, be ye steadfast, unmovable, always abounding in the work of the Lord, forasmuch as ye know that your labour is not in vain in the Lord (1 Cor. 15:58).

God Assessment Perspective

I need you to answer the following questions before you continue reading this book. The following information needs to be clarified before you can honestly approach this work objectively:

1) Is the God of your faith all-powerful, all-knowing, and everywhere *all* the time? (yes or no)
2. Is the God of your faith flawless or perfect? (yes or no)
3. Would the God of your faith lie? (yes or no)
4. Would the God of your faith exaggerate matters? (yes or no)
5. Could the God of your faith miss the mark? (yes or no)
6. From your limited understanding, do you believe everything God allowed to be written in the Holy Bible is true? (yes or no)
7. Is the God your faith the same God spoken of in the Holy Bible? (yes or no)
8) Is anything too hard for your God? (yes or no)

If you answered incorrectly, go and reevaluate who your god is (little *g*) and then continue reading. In order to receive the information in this book, you must first believe that the God of the Holy Bible is real and is *always* in control! With each section of this book, it is imperative that you reflect back to this assessment in order to keep things in perspective.

Answer key: 1 = Y, 2 = Y, 3 = N, 4 = N, 5 = N, 6 = Y, 7 = Y, 8 = N.

Chapter 1

God's Power and Wisdom

The Bible begins in the book of Genesis, which states, "In the beginning God created the heaven and the earth. And the earth was without form, and void" (Gen. 1:1–2). There is a doctrinal teaching that the earth was in a chaotic mess because of the word *void*. The word can also mean "emptiness" or "state of chaos." Even if we accept both definitions, we must first put them in perspective of *who* they are associated with. If you know and understand who God is, then you would understand that *He is perfect* and what He speaks is perfect. If we read God's word as a natural man, then we might interpret this encounter as a "chaotic mess." However, when we look at it from a spiritual standpoint and understanding who God is, then we understand that "without form" means nothing was placed on earth as yet, therefore "void" or "empty." A chaotic mess denotes total disorganization as well as lack of purpose. Anyone who knows or understands God just a little will know this is all contrary to His character. People's faith in God tends to waiver because God is presented in many ways contrary to who He really is! Because of His magnificence, it's really hard to describe who He is without making Him somewhat limited as we are. At any rate, we need to check what we anticipate saying before we just throw it out there. We should not just comment on everything. Solomon once scribed there's "a time to keep silence, and a time to speak" (Eccl. 3:7). We, as ministers of the gospel, should put this into action more often.

While we don't know the time span between when God created the heaven and the earth and when He created the first night and day, we do know that when God speaks, His words *always* accomplish what they're set forth to accomplish (Isa. 55:11). When it comes to things in time, God knows the end from the beginning. I'm not saying He doesn't know things outside of time because He does! However, for the sake of clarity on this topic, we *must* keep in mind that time as we know it did not exist until God created the heavens and the earth. When God spoke something into existence, it was! Why? Because He believed that it would be so. He didn't doubt what the result would be, but believed the result before the statement. This is ultimate faith! Now if you understand this, then you should understand what the writer of Hebrews 11:3 meant. It is not our faith we stand on to believe that the worlds were framed by the word of God but through God's faith. Why not our faith? I'm glad you asked! It would not be faith for us because we see the creations. According to Hebrews 11:1, "Now faith is the substance of things hoped for, the *evidence* of things *not seen*." As a result, God spoke things into existence that were not, as though they were; and the scripture tells us over and over again, "and it was so!" God did not step back after He created a thing and say, "Shoot, I messed that up! Let me try this." No! God said it, and it was so!

Before we can truly begin to understand God and the scriptures He inspired to be written, we must first yield to His power, and don't deviate. What do I mean? I'm glad you asked. You can't say in one breath that God is all-knowing but make statements as if God didn't know what was coming out of left field in the next breath.

Doctrine: When God created the heaven and the earth, the earth was in a chaotic mess, there was darkness all around, and it was cold so nothing could survive.

Let me ask a few questions. What came first, the chicken or the egg, the man or the baby, the tree or the seed? While we shouldn't read the Bible as a book, some things God just makes simple and plain. You can't view every scripture as something deep and mysterious as though you're looking to crack God's secret since the foundation of time! I have no doubt there are still applications of God's word we have yet to unveil, however, they shouldn't deviate from God's initial interpretation.

Truth: When God created the heaven and the earth, it was perfect in its initial state. Yes, there was nothing else formed on it at its conception, but it was complete and perfect as it was!

At the end of each day of creation, God said, "It is good!" What does that honestly mean to you? Does it only mean, "That's okay," "It's Cool," "That's all right," or "That'll do"? Take a minute, and think about what that means to you.

Remember in Isaiah 55:11, God was saying that *whatever* He speaks will go out and accomplish exactly what he intended it to accomplish. It will never return void! In other words, it will never return empty or without success. It will always prosper or be successful. If the word is to destroy, then it will be prosperous or successful in the destruction. If it is a blessing, then it will be prosperous or successful in its blessing. No matter the outcome, it *will* accomplish exactly what it was intended for. *Hmmm!* Now one could say this is a doctrinal teaching. This is just scripture without any twists, not a motive to be considered a deep thinker. This is just scripture without *any* additives. You see, God is all that and a bag of chips! This has absolutely nothing to do with the Hebrew or Aramaic translation. This is about keeping God where He belongs and staying consistent with our belief. It is absolutely imperative that you believe God is all that before you can move on to some of God's more complex attributes. The God that the scriptures talk about is the same God Christianity is built upon. He is *all powerful* yet *merciful!* Psalm 136 tells us to give thanks to the Lord our God "for He is good!" It tells us over and over again "For his mercy endureth forever." It tells me He is "the God of gods," He "alone doeth great wonders," His "wisdom made the heavens," He "made great light," He made "the sun to rule by day" and "the moon and stars to rule by night," He delivered Israel out of Egypt,; He overthrew Pharaoh and slew famous kings,

He "remembered us in our low estate," He "redeemed us from our enemies," and He "giveth food to all flesh." Why??? "For *his* mercy endureth forever!"

Now some would like to put God in a box and place limitations on Him. Some would even question God's motives as if they actually possessed full understanding. To actually be in that state of mind puts an individual on the same plane as God. This would only get the same response from God that Job had in Job 38. God, who drew up the blueprints, would ask, "Where were you when I laid the foundations of the earth?" God would ask you who drew up the blue prints if you know? God would ask you what those foundations are attached to ("or who laid the corner stone thereof"). God may ask you, "who shut up the sea with doors, when it brake forth, as if it had issued out of the womb?" (Job 38:8). God may ask you where you were when He decreed the limits by which the waters of the sea could flow and their waves had limitations of how far they could go. God may ask you if you commanded when morning would be since you were born (Job. 38:12). God may ask you if death obeys you or if you've seen and known the presence of death. God may ask if you know "the breadth of the earth" (Job 38:18). God may ask you if you know where the light dwells or even the darkness. Where do they go when you don't see them? God may ask you if you know riches in the concept of snow or hail. God may ask if you understand the dynamics of lightning and thunder, which may "cause it to rain on the earth, where no man is" (Job 38:26). God may ask, "Hath the rain a father? or who hath begotten the drops of dew?" (Job 38:28). God may ask you, "Who hath put wisdom in the inward parts? or who hath given understanding to the heart?" (Job 38:36). These are just a few things God could ask you. God once stated in Job 41:11, "whatsoever is under the *whole* heaven is mine."

So do you truly believe that God has power to create everything we see? Do you truly believe God understands how everything that *He* created works? Do you really believe He set the stars, moons, and planets in place? Does He have that kind of power? Do you really believe He has the understanding of how to make it so that the water on earth doesn't overflow their banks? Do you really believe

God knows our tomorrow? Do you really believe God is omnipotent, omnipresent, and omniscient? *Hmmm!*

We find in James 1:5, "If any of you lack wisdom, let him ask of God, that giveth to all men liberally, and upbraideth not; and it *shall* be given him." Hopefully, you prayed and asked God to open your understanding before you began reading this book. If you didn't, then pray now for God to show you what He meant to be understood. Proverbs 4:7 says, "Wisdom is the principal thing; therefore get wisdom: and with all thy getting get understanding." I hope I've laid a sufficient amount of information to establish a foundation conducive for understanding part of God's true character. Understanding God's ultimate power is paramount to understanding man's position in God's plan as it even relates to Jesus Christ. If you don't fully understand what has already been stated, the next chapter may prove to be a bit complex. Nevertheless, it is God who brings understanding through the Holy Spirit. I pray that you would allow the Holy Spirit to fill you with understanding and all things necessary for your spiritual growth.

From this point on, you *must* keep in mind that God makes no mistakes and He is aware of *everything*. Without this understanding, you will put God back in your little box and limit His *true* majesty! Not only that, but there is *no* way you could continue reading this book of truths with understanding. You *must* understand that the **absolute** *greatest* thing you think God could do would only scratch the surface of who God really is! Even men with the greatest minds throughout history and in modern times, man's wisdom and understanding is so finite in comparison to my God's infinite wisdom and understanding that there are no words or terms to describe the differences. If you have decided to read on, I know God will bless our understanding of Him. He is always pleased when we try to know Him more. For some, this may be a refresher; for others, an awakening. Regardless of your position, remember there is nothing new under the sun, some things are just being illuminated in our understanding. Finally, keep in mind who God is not from a limited viewpoint. Our greatest thought of God's capability only scratches the surface of what God can actually do!

Chapter 2

The Eden Experience

Chapter 1 laid the foundation for the understanding of God's power and wisdom. In order to get a complete understanding of God's dealings with mankind according to scripture, it is imperative you read *all* the scriptures! You need to read and study the entire Bible. You cannot truly consider yourself a seasoned or mature minister of God's word if you have not ever read God's word in its entirety. One might say, "That's not true because I've been a minister or pastor for years and I've never read the Bible in its entirety." *Hmmm!* Exactly what is the health of your flock spiritually? Are they still struggling with the milk of God's word? Most likely they are. It could possibly be because, truth be told, a lot of what you teach is only milk-based. While milk is very nutritious, it's mainly for babies. After a certain age, it becomes detrimental to the health of the individual because it no longer provides the nutrients needed to sustain growth. Paul speaks to the Christians at Corinth who were carnal, babes in Christ who were on the milk of the word (1 Cor. 3:1–4). The author of Hebrews also talks about those who can only handle the milk of the word because the meat was for those who are skillful in the word. The writer alludes that they should be on the meat as long as they've been in Christ, but were not (Heb. 5:11–6:3)

Spiritual meat comes with a thorough diet of God's word. When you eat the smorgasbord of food spread at the table, you get nutrients you never knew about, strengthening you more and more as you consume more and more. You go from milk to soft veggies, soft proteins to more solid food. Your digestive system starts developing. Eventually you can move to all solids and some liquids to help the process along. Our spiritual man requires the same process in order to grow and mature. This is accomplished by consuming the whole word of God. The beautiful thing is that God gives us the nutrients we need from His word as we continue to ingest them. However, we can't stay in the same area and expect to grow. That would be like only eating lettuce from the garden and expecting your muscles to grow, which requires protein. Guess what? It's not going to happen! So you must intake the complete diet of God's word and trust His Holy Spirit will dispense to you nutrients you need in order to grow.

Now hear this, I can't trust man to give me what God has for me so I have to get it for myself. In other words, I can't go to church on Sunday and expect to be nourished for the rest of the week. But what you receive on Sunday may only be an appetizer to the main course God has for you throughout the week. You need to ingest God's word daily in order to grow. Remember, the Bereans searched the scriptures daily (Acts 17:11)

The word of God is to man what computer software is to a computer. If there is no software downloaded into your computer, you have nothing to pull up to interface with in order to solve a problem. Likewise, if you never pour God's word into your spirit man, the Holy Spirit has nothing to draw from in order to bring anything to your remembrance because there is nothing there. However, if you pour God's complete word in, then the Holy Spirit has a wealth of information to pull from. Even though you may not understand at the time you've studied or read the word, God gives the understanding when it's needed. At what point in your walk of faith do you become obedient to God's word? Paul states in 2 Timothy 2:15, "Study to shew thyself approved unto God, a workman that needeth not to be ashamed, rightly dividing the word of truth."

Now there are those who can break this down from Greek and give you a fifteen-page dissertation on this scripture I'm sure. Nevertheless, the bottom line is that if you want God to approve you; then study His word. In doing this, you won't have to be ashamed that you can't spiritually speak on any subject related to God. It's not you who brings clarity to any subject anyway, but the Holy Spirit. Christ told us in John 14:26 that "the Comforter, which is the Holy Ghost, whom the Father will send in my name, he shall teach you all things, and bring all things to your *remembrance*, whatsoever I have said unto you." However, if you've never read God's word, then the Holy Ghost will have nothing to bring to your remembrance! I'll say that again. If you never read God's word to be taught of the Holy Ghost, then the Holy Ghost will have nothing to bring to your remembrance! Commentaries are fine to give you some direction at times. However, your whole theology of scripture should *never* rest on something you've gotten from a commentary. You have to search the scripture yourself to rightly divide the word. Not every commentary is factual or spiritual. Not every commentary is a direct revelation from God. Just like not every instructor in seminary school is spirit-filled. We find in Acts 17:11 that "those in Thessalonica" were not as noble as those of Berea because the Bereans "received the word with all readiness of mind, and searched the scriptures daily, whether those things were so." So whatever you are taught—whether by reading, hearing, or watching—you should *always* search the scripture to see if what's stated is truth.

Doctrine: The Fall of Man
Some say Adam was weak because he let Satan get all in Eve's ear. They say Adam was standing right there with Eve and never said a word. Then they say Adam tried to blame the woman.

Those teaching this doctrine are looking at this from a carnal viewpoint. Prior to Eve's encounter, there was no sin in mankind so Adam would have no reason to think deception. This being the case, you have to change your whole mind-set. Now I've heard this doctrine taught by many, and it always ends the same! Men need to take accountability for their actions and quit making excuses like Adam. They say God told Adam not to eat the forbidden fruit and never told Eve. Therefore, Adam was ultimately responsible because he should have known better. Well, take a stroll with me a moment and let me lay some *truth* on you!

According to the progression of scripture, God created animal life before mankind. Now we find this in Genesis 1:24–27. When God decided to create man, He made him much like Himself. In many respects, God made man in accordance to *Their* image and in accordance after *Their* likeness. Notice I said "Their," which is plural. Not only that, but man would have dominion over everything on earth! God rules *everything everywhere*, and He gave man this same similar rule on Earth. Genesis 1:28 states, God blessed them and gave them rule over everything on earth. There was no fear of anything because mankind had dominion and rule. At this time, mankind and animals alike were *all* vegetarians. Therefore, nothing was killed for food as God had given the green herbs of the field for food to man and animals (Gen. 1:29–30). Understanding this, we see there was *no* violence, deceit, or corruption at that time. Everything flowed in harmony. Everyone accepted their place. The lions weren't eating the lambs, the birds weren't eating the fish, and man was not eating any of the animals. *Harmony!*

Now just because the scripture we read runs progressively doesn't mean this is the order of progression. We can't read the scripture with the comprehension of a book as this would be with the natural mind. According to Paul, the natural man cannot receive things that are spiritual because they wouldn't make sense (1 Cor. 2:14). What do I mean? I'm glad you asked! Well, according to Genesis 1:24–25, God creates the animals. In Genesis 1:27, God created man. In Genesis 1:28, God told Adam and Eve to be fruitful and multiply. Then Genesis 2:7 shows how God created man. Genesis 2:18 shows man alone. Then Genesis 2:19 shows God creating the animals and then bringing them to Adam to name them. Genesis 2:20 shows Adam naming everything but then realized he doesn't have a mate for himself like all the other animals. However, Adam was told in the previous chapter to multiply and populate the earth (Gen. 1:28). Nevertheless, we see woman made in Genesis 2:21–23, and Adam is satisfied. At this point, the man and his wife were to be considered *one* flesh. The truth be told, she was literally part of man as she was *made* from him. Now a lot of scripture can be understood in the natural progression, but even with that, you still have to ask God for clarity.

Hopefully at this point, you can see how God has created man in His image and after His likeness. God's character is descriptive of possessing wisdom and power in order to direct and protect. These attributes were also a part of Adam's DNA because that's how God created him. It is absolutely imperative that you understand this was part of Adam's DNA. Similarly, because Eve was made from Adam, this was also part of her DNA. We see this in men and women even today. Men, for the most part, want to protect their family while women want to protect their children. It may seem insignificant on the surface but as you begin to put it *all* in perspective, it is really huge. You will hopefully see what I mean by huge as we continue. Now we see Eve being approached by the serpent in Genesis 3:1–5. Doctrinal teachings will lead you to believe that Adam was present during Eve's conversation with the serpent. However, not only does the scripture *not* state that, but it never remotely alludes to that point. We do know that Adam had the responsibility of working in the garden eastward of Eden. We don't know where Eve was in the garden when she had her conversation with the serpent as it was *never* referenced. However, we do know she was somewhere near the middle of the garden because that's where the tree of life was and the tree of knowledge of good and evil (Gen. 2:9). What we do know is that her conversation ended at Genesis 3:5. There are even some who say Eve didn't know about not eating the fruit. However, she quoted in Genesis 3:3 what God had stated in Genesis 2:17, but also added they weren't allowed to even touch it! Therefore, scripture shows that Eve was very much aware of the consequences. Paul understood that the fall of man was the result of the woman being deceived, not Adam (1 Tim. 2:14). No matter how hard some may want to believe that Adam is responsible in order to come up with a reason to get men under submission, just stick to pure scripture. God does not need help to get mankind to conform to His scripture. His pure unadulterated word is enough when rightly divided. They are both responsible, but we need to understand the perspective of their individual responsibility as it refers to the fall.

Now allow the Holy Spirit to open your understanding regarding the fall of man. Because of mankind's sin, God made the first blood sacrifice for mankind in order to clothe them (Gen. 3:21). Now is the time to get to the meat of this downfall and understand the *redemptive* power of God. It will be easier to work from the end back to the beginning. Remember that our God already knows the end from the beginning. There is a really good reason Adam is held in comparison to Jesus, but the greater part of scholars and such have yet to understand this. Remember, there is nothing new under the sun. This is not a new revelation. Some are just now seeing the light. Jesus died so that we would be able to have abundant life. Because of mankind's sin, God required a blood sacrifice be made to atone for our sin (Exod. 29:36). Before God gave the law of blood sacrifices, He made the first sacrifice in Genesis 3:21. Jesus gave Himself as the final ultimate sacrifice so that we could have access to the Father (Heb. 9:24–26). Because of Adam, everyone eventually dies; but because of Christ, everyone has the chance to live (1 Cor. 15:22). God made the first sacrifice because of man's sin, and God (Christ) made the final sacrifice for man's sin. The alpha and omega, the beginning and the end. Christ gave Himself so that we could all live. When I say "all," I'm speaking of the church, the bride of Christ. Have you ever really wondered why? Paul wrote in Ephesians 5:25, "Husbands, *love* our wives, even as Christ also loved the church, and gave himself for it." *Hmmm!* I'm glad you asked! Have you ever wondered why?

Now 2 Timothy 3:16–17 states, "All scripture is given by inspiration of God, and is profitable for doctrine, for reproof, for correction, for instruction in righteousness: that the man of God may be perfect, *thoroughly* furnished unto all good works." You can't accept one part of scripture because it helps you make a point and then intentionally ignore the other parts of scripture because it doesn't agree with the point you'd like to make. Remember, God is not the author of confusion (1 Cor. 14:33).

Now, we understand the end of how Christ loved us so much that he sacrificed Himself to give us life. It is often said that the Old

Testament is God's plan concealed while the New Testament is God's word revealed. Because man was made in the *likeness* of God, he possessed the same character as God. Was man equal to God? No, of course not! Man was the *image* of God (Gen. 1:26–27), but man is not God, but only a likeness of God! Most of us understand that because sin is *not* a part of God, then anything that is a part of sin cannot dwell in the presence of God. Therefore, man in his natural state cannot dwell in the presence of God. Sacrifices were a bridge for man to come back in the presence of God. However, they were only temporary because there had to be death before life was given. Christ became our *final* sacrifice before we could obtain everlasting life! Christ was that bridge that will never be broken. Christ knew the consequences of sacrifice! He knew the pain and agony He'd have to endure. He knew from a human standpoint the humiliation He would have to go through yet He went through it anyway! Why? I'm glad you asked! In the event they would change their mind, they would have a way back. That's *love!*

Adam knew that after Eve touched the fruit, she would die, let alone to eat it. How do we know? I'm glad you asked! According to Genesis 2:17 and Genesis 3:3, they knew the consequences. You see, Adam knew that if Eve disobeyed God, her fate would be death! To this point, according to scripture, death here meant the end of fellowship with God. We see this in Genesis 3:9 as Adam tried to hide. Because of the *love* Adam had for Eve, he willingly gave himself to receive the penalty of death. Get this, Adam accepted Eve as literally part of him and received the charge that they should be considered *one* flesh. This is why Adam said in Genesis 2:23, "This is now bone of my bones, and flesh of my flesh." He knew she literally came from him! Now the question to husbands would be, do you love your wife enough to lay down your life for her? *Hmmm!* We've read what Ephesians 5:25 said regarding loving your wife as Christ loved the church and gave Himself for it. We find through scripture that Adam was "the figure of him that was to come" (Rom. 5:14). Because of Adam's disobedience, all were condemned; but through Christ, all were made righteous (Rom. 5:19). In your spare time, read Romans 5:12–21.

Adam's love was so pure that he sacrificed his *life* for one (Eve) to take upon death. Christ's love was so pure that He *died* for all the world to receive life (1 Cor. 15:22). This is ultimate love! Jesus told us in John 15:13, "Greater love hath no man than this, that a man lay down his life for his friends." What Adam did for his wife was excellent! What Christ did was *great* for mankind, whom He considered His friends! Adam's love for Eve (his bride) was a foreshadow of the love Christ has for the church (His bride). Adam was not a dummy or an ignorant man, as some have painted him to be. No, Adam had an *agape* love for Eve that was truly 'til death do we part! Because of this example, Paul told men to love their wives "even as Christ also loved the church, and gave himself for it." Christ literally died for the church! Men should love their wife just as Adam loved Eve, but more so like Christ loved the church. Hence, according to 1 Corinthians 15:45, 47, "The first man Adam was made a living soul; the last Adam was made a quickening spirit... The first man is of the earth, earthy: the second man is the Lord from heaven."

I initially gave you the doctrine, now you have the truth!

Truth: Adam was everything but weak, passive, or irresponsible. Adam gave of himself in order that mankind (Eve) would not suffer alone.

You see, God *always* knows the end from the beginning. Remember, God created man after His likeness and after His image. That should tell you something! Adam was to Eve what Christ is to the church. "Greater love hath no man than this, that a man lay down his life for his friends" (Jn. 15:13).

A minister of god's word should never feel they have to fluff God's word to try and make a point. God's word is strong enough to stand on its own. A student of God's word has to have the Holy Spirit to help them articulate what God wants to be conveyed. The Holy Spirit knows everything from Genesis to Revelation and doesn't have to think or rethink what the Father meant. The key to this for *any* minister or student of God's word is that they *must* spend time in God's word in order to build a library of information the Holy Spirit can work with. Again, the Holy Spirit can't bring anything to your "remembrance" if you don't have anything to remember. One of the other things to remember is that in studying God's word, you will never necessarily understand everything you read the first, second, third, etc., time through. God gives you what you need for the time and season you're in at the moment. Your memory is built from there. Well-known ministers, such as the Apostle LaFayette Scales, Bishop T. D. Jakes, or the renowned Miles Monroe did not acquire their understanding overnight but over time! As you show yourself approved unto God, He gives you more and more. Solomon said in Ecclesiastes 3:1, "To every thing there is a season, and a time to every purpose under the heaven:" Everything under the sun (or Son) has a season, time, and purpose according to God's plan.

Allow God to minister to you as you feed on His word. Allow the Holy Spirit to help you grow as you move on to a better understanding of God's word. Don't worry about how much the other minister, pastor, evangelist, teacher, etc., knows. Appreciate what God has given you. Trust me, you will receive a revelation others don't have yet, but only because that's what God had for you in your season. God may want you to be the vessel in a given season to deliver a word. Remember, don't use the same cup every time you want a drink!

Chapter 3

Jesus and the Father

As we read and study God's word, we should get to the point where we know the truth from a false understanding when we hear it. Again, you will be able to distinguish these differences if you have spent time in God's word and prayed for clarity. Otherwise, you will believe most anything you're taught. You should *never* stop having that Berean mentality that receives a teaching with an open mind but then goes back to search the scriptures to see if what is being taught is truly what the Lord is saying (Acts 17:11).

The first two chapters covered controversial topics of doctrinal teachings. This chapter doesn't fall short of controversy either, but is most never covered in detail. I'm not giving something new in terms of understanding as there are others who hold the same understanding. I'm just putting it on paper because this is what God has given me to scribe.

Doctrine: There is no difference between Jesus and the Father. They are both God. We will see in the end. It's not meant for us to understand now!

I can kind of understand how this might be somewhat difficult to grasp. However, after spending time in God's word, it became clearer there were obvious differences. It has been said that the Godhead is similar to time, as you have past, present, and future.

With an egg, you have the shell, yoke, and the membrane or white. Even with mankind, you have body, soul, and spirit. Some might even refute these analogies that the Godhead is deeper than that and we can't use these types of analogies. Why not? At least, they give you a starting point of possibilities. Some would like to think they're just so deep and reject these simple examples. Nevertheless, they can't even give you something remotely close or a scripture to support their rejection. God has taken the foolish or simple things to confound the wise (1 Cor. 1:27). So is there a scripture reference to support they are distinctively different yet the same? *Hmmm!* I'm glad you asked!

While there are many scriptures to support this stand, we will only cover a few good ones. In the beginning of time, we see that God created the heaven and earth (Gen. 1:1). Then we see the Spirit of God moving "upon the face of the waters" (Gen. 1:2) Then we see the Godhead communing together as they said in Genesis 1:26, "And God said, let us make man in our image, after our likeness." After this, we see the Lord God making man from the dust of the ground (Gen. 2:7). In creation, we see the Godhead working together and acting individually.

If we fast-forward to the New Testament, the beloved disciple breaks it down like this in John 1:1, "In the beginning was the Word, and the Word was with God, and the Word was God." John speaks of Him separately, being *with* God, and then as *actually* being God! John then goes on to tell us that God created everything (John 1:3). Even Paul speaks of the Father and Son in creation. Paul tells us in Colossians 1:12–17 that the Father delivered us from the power of darkness and transplanted us into the kingdom of His Son. Then Paul says the Son is the image of the invisible God, by Him everything was created in heaven and earth and were created for Him. Finally, John tells us that Jesus became a fleshly man (John 1:14). Now we see part of the Godhead becoming mankind. Some might say that all God did was made Himself flesh and left heaven temporarily to redeem mankind. It was still just the one and same God. Is that so? *Hmmm!*

Jesus was here on earth roughly thirty years before He was baptized. When Jesus was baptized, we see the Godhead functioning individually at the *same* time. Matthew 3:16–17 states, "And Jesus, when he was baptized...*saw* the Spirit of God descending like a dove, and lighting upon him: And lo a voice from heaven, saying, This is my beloved Son, in whom I am well pleased." Now if nothing else convinces you they are distinctively different, this passage should. Just because they're different doesn't take away from the fact they're still one. Jesus says in John 10:30, "I and my Father are one." Jesus even takes it a step further when Philip asks to see the Father. Jesus said in John 14:9, "he that hath seen me hath seen the Father." Even so, Jesus brings a subtle clarity to what He means in John 14:10 when He says, "I am in the Father, and the Father in me?...the Father that dwelleth in me." Some get tied up in the statement, "I and the Father are one" and don't see the clarity Jesus has given. This is also how many are led astray.

John is an excellent book to see the individuality as well as the collective unity of the Godhead. Jesus goes on in that same John chapter 14 to give further proof of the Godhead. In John 14:16, Jesus said, "And I will pray the Father, and he shall give you another Comforter." Then He goes on to state in John 14:26, "But the Comforter, which is the Holy Ghost, whom the Father will send in my name." Even though they are individual, they are still collectively God! Jesus says back in John 8:28, "I do nothing of myself; but as my Father hath taught me." Over and over, Jesus speaks of the Father apart from Himself and in unity with Him.

Let's move on. In Revelation 5:5–7, we see Christ and the Father in operation. "The Lion of the tribe of Judah, the Root of David...stood a Lamb as it had been slain... And he came and took the book out the right hand of him that sat upon the throne." You see, even in the Godhead, there is a hierarchy of authority. That may have hit some pretty hard! Nevertheless, the scripture is the scripture. You have to take it all! You can't just take what you *think* will make a good message. You can't cut and paste God's word to make yourself look good or to present yourself to be something you're not! It's okay if you didn't know, and then you receive understanding. At any rate, when you do come into the knowledge of truth, you need to correct those you've mislead. An influential man once said a good teacher is one who can still be taught. We are not above being taught, and it doesn't matter how long we've been teaching! God's word is awesome and true. You can't just stand on part of it and kick the other parts to the curb. How about Revelation 1:1? It states, "The Revelation of Jesus Christ, which God (the Father) *gave* unto him (Jesus), to shew unto his (Jesus') servants things which must shortly come to pass; and he (Jesus) sent and signified it by his (Jesus) angel unto his (Jesus) servant John." You see, Jesus received a revelation of the Father. Some might say that's crazy! You're playing on scripture! Where else can you see something like that? *Hmmm!* I'm glad you asked! Jesus was asked about the end of days and His second coming. Jesus gives a lot of information in Mark13 but makes a profound statement in Mark 13:32, "But of that day and that hour knoweth no man, no, not the angels which are in heaven, neither the Son, but the Father." This doesn't take anything from who Jesus is. But for those who can't seem to fully grasp the Godhead, this should put you on track to now broaden your scope of understanding the magnificence of God. Just when you think God can be put in your little box, He gives you another dimension of understanding.

Let me help someone here. Many commentaries can be fine, but you can *never* base your total understanding of God's word from commentaries. Why not? *Hmmm!* I'm glad you asked! Well, not every commentary is written by the guidance of the Holy Spirit. Everyone who writes a commentary isn't necessarily Spirit-filled, just like not everyone teaching in a seminary school is Spirit-filled! You can spit out history all day to me and it may be somewhat accurate, however, if you can't give the spiritual purpose of that history, it's just good historical information. I'm talking about biblical history. At any rate, commentaries are fine, but you still need to research the validity of the information. Just like the Bereans, you must search to see if those things are so.

At this point, if nothing has enlightened you regarding the Godhead and Their hierarchy, chew on this next point. God gave Paul a profound understanding of the hierarchy of the Godhead when he scribed in 1 Corinthians 15:20–28, "But now is Christ risen from the dead, and become the first fruits of them that slept... For in

Adam all die, even so in Christ shall all be made alive. But every man in his own order... Then cometh the end, when he (Jesus) shall have delivered up the kingdom to God, even the Father... For he (Jesus) must reign, till he hath put all enemies under his feet... And when all things shall be subdued unto him, then shall the Son also himself be subject unto him (the Father) that put all things under him, that God may be all in all." So you see, though the Son has all power and authority, He will ultimately give it back to the Father who gave it to Him. This will be done so that the Godhead can once again be "all in all."

> *Truth: There is a difference in the Father and Son. They are both God but from the standpoint of functioning as one. And last, it is meant for us to understand! Just because you don't understand something doesn't mean it's not for us to understand!*

Though there are countless other scriptures we could have used, we've only given those that were essential to jump-starting ones spiritual understanding. As we alluded to early on, God is so magnificently wonderful, there is nothing too hard for Him (Them). Now having said that, it should still be understood that there is still *only one* God, not three. Do not let the threefold manifestation of His being throw you off. Just remember, you have a body, soul, and spirit (Heb. 4:12). Also remember, "God said, let us make man in our image, and after our likeness" (Gen. 1:26). In most aspects, just as God is, we are. If you can understand your physical and spiritual makeup, then it should make it easier to understand the Godhead. Again, pray if you need more clarity. "If any of you lack wisdom, let him ask of God, that giveth to all men liberally, and upbraideth not; and it shall be given him" (Jas. 1:5)

Chapter 4

Apostles and Prophets

This chapter covers a subject that I'm sure will be attacked…to say the least. This is a subject that shows as much controversy in our time as the Messiah walking and talking in the days Jesus walked the earth. What do I mean? Hmmmm! I'm glad you asked! In the days Jesus walked the earth, the chief priests and Pharisees thought that there was no way God would send someone of Jesus' status to lead the children of Israel, that God just didn't operate like that. Keep in mind that they had all the scripture necessary to confirm his identity. Nevertheless, they were like the husbandmen Jesus spoke about in the parable in Matthew 21:33–46. Today, we have much that same mentality amongst the pastors, teachers, and preachers. In many things, they are as separated among themselves as the Pharisees and Sadducees were. Excluding all the books written by popular men as well as all the commentaries in the world, simply ask yourself the only important question, what does God's word say?

If you lack an understanding of God's word, then ask Him! We're told in James 1:5, "If any of you lack wisdom, let him ask of God, that giveth to all men liberally, and upbraideth not; and it shall be given him." By no means I am saying to ignore books and commentaries because, in many cases, they were given to men by God to be written. However, I am encouraging you to first seek God for an understanding.

Doctrine: There are no more apostles or prophets today.

If this is your belief, it's fine because it's your belief. God gave us all a mind of our own so we could choose what we wish. However, if we search the scripture as God gives us an understanding, we will see things in a different light. If you truly believe the Bible is the word of God, then you would sincerely believe what Timothy wrote in 2 Timothy 3:16–17, "All scripture is given by inspiration of God, and is profitable for doctrine, for reproof, for correction, for instruction in righteousness: That the man of God may be perfect, thoroughly furnished unto all good works." When this scripture says "all," it means to the inclusion of *everything*, and to the exclusion of *nothing*! Therefore, this encompasses the complete Bible. Now let's take a look at a passage written by Paul in an epistle to the Ephesians:

> *And he gave some, apostles; and some, prophets; and some, evangelists; and some, pastors and teachers; For perfecting of the saints, for the work of the ministry, for the edifying of the body of Christ: Till we all come in the unity of the faith, and of the knowledge of the Son of God, unto a perfect man, unto the measure of the stature of the fullness of Christ: That we henceforth be no more children, tossed to and fro, and carried about with every wind of doctrine, by the sleight of men, and cunning craftiness, whereby they lie in wait to deceive; But speaking the truth in love, may grow up into him in all things, which is the head, even Christ: From whom the whole body fitly joined together and compacted by that which every joint supplieth, according to the effectual working in the measure of every part, maketh increase of the body unto the edifying of itself in love. (Eph. 4:11–16)*

One of the key words in this passage is *till*! First, understand that Christ has already been crucified, buried, and risen. Therefore, this scripture was written about the church roughly thirty years *after* Christ's resurrection. As a result of this, anything written would pertain to the church, the body of Christ! If you don't understand this point, then take a moment to meditate on that fact and ask God to give you clarity. This word *till* is important because it denotes a time line of sorts. What do I mean? I'm glad you asked! This word gives us parameters of operation. "You can do this or that till I come again" or "You can play till it's dark" or |You can proceed till you see such and such sign" or "You will have this blessing till you transgress my law" or "Peter walked on water till he doubted," etc I'll give this to the body till such a time. The meaning of this word never changes, and never has, no matter what language it's used in.

There are many who don't accept this scripture in its entirety because they're not walking by faith, but by sight. Either that or they've been *taught* something different. If it's neither of these reasons, then it's because they've never really searched the scripture for clarity. You see, God takes the simple things to confound the wise. Remember, because you don't understand something, doesn't mean it's not so. When it comes to scripture, you may not understand everything you read the first, second, or third time around, but God gives us understanding as necessary for our spiritual growth. Therefore, if something doesn't sit right in your spirit, keep silent and ponder it in your spirit. Ask God to bring clarity and don't move to the right or left until He's given you instruction to move. Remember, there's a time for everything.

Moving on, what is an Apostle? Some say an Apostle is one who walked with Christ during His earthly ministry. Others say an Apostle had to be chosen by Christ. Some even say that there could have only been twelve Apostles, because that's who Jesus chose. Nevertheless, the term *Apostle* has several noted meanings, but one widely agreed upon is "one sent forth." While we are all familiar with the initial twelve Apostles, there were others mentioned but not often referenced. Justus and Matthias were mentioned in Acts 1:23–26 who walked with Jesus during His earthly ministry. Paul and Barnabas were mentioned as Apostles in Acts 14:14. Andronicus and Junia were mentioned in Romans 16:7. Now what do these men, in addition to the known twelve Apostles, have in common? They were all commissioned to establish the church, the body of Christ. More so of Paul, Silas, and others that we see them establishing churches. That is not to say that Peter and the others didn't, but that we have more documentation in the scripture of Paul and his companions primarily because Paul wrote more epistles than anyone, according to the complete work that we have in the Bible. Nonetheless, an Apostle is one sent by God to establish His church.

Okay then, so Jesus was an Apostle for God the Father! In John 17:3, we find Jesus speaking with the Father and speaks of Himself in relation to the Father, stating, "whom thou hast sent." Jesus even states in John 20:21, "as my Father hath sent me, even so send I you." One may ask now, how are you going to demote Christ to being an Apostle? I'm not demoting Christ, only bringing clarity to a term. Have you not read what the author of Hebrews scribed in Hebrews 3:1 "Wherefore, holy brethren, partakers of the heavenly calling, consider the *apostle* and *high priest* of our profession, Christ Jesus; who was faithful to Him that appointed Him." *Boom!* Jesus was sent to reconcile/redeem mankind back to the living God.

Apostles were sent to establish the church, group of believers, who would trust and receive that available redemption. It really doesn't matter if you feel better ascribing or associating the original Twelve with a capital *A*, and all others with a lowercase *a*. The Bible does not differentiate the two groups. All we know is those who would be accounted with the board of directors had to have actually walked with Christ in His earthly ministry. Just remember that an apostle is one who has been *sent* to establish! Ask yourself this, are churches still being established? Are the lost still being converted? Is God still calling people to establish and convert the lost?

Moving right along, what is a prophet? This is just as controversial as that of the question of the existence of an Apostle. A prophet is simply one who proclaims a divine word sent direct from the throne of God. This could be a word of something to come, or something already accomplished yet to be revealed. Prophesy isn't just of those things Christ was to accomplish. We need to quit putting God in a box. Quit accepting just a part of God's word and accept the *whole* word of God. You can't mix up Prophecy and the office of a Prophet. They are not the same or interchangeable. The word *prophecy* in scripture has two different meanings, for the most part, from the Old and New Testaments. The Old Testament speaks of that which was to come to past while the New Testament mostly refers to instructive *preaching*! Now there are two different spellings. *Prophecy* refers to that which is to come and *prophesy* refers to an instructive word. According to *Vine's Expository Dictionary of New Testament Words*, they both signify "the speaking forth of the mind and counsel of God." Therefore, if I see *prophecy*, I know it is in relation to future events. If I see *prophesy* or *prophesying*, I know it refers to speak or speaking! When you read God's word, don't just read it like a regular book. Listen as you read. God gave us commas, colons, semicolons, periods, etc., for a reason. Listen as you read, and you'll hear what God is saying.

Is God still speaking today? Of course He is! Are there still things God wants to reveal to man today? Of course there are! Have you fulfilled your purpose today? Of course not because you're reading this now! If your purpose has been completed, then God will take you home because your mission has been accomplished. There would be no reason for you to remain here. Therefore, if the mission is not accomplished, then there are still things to be accomplished. Some people receive a word from God through other people some would be considered prophets. These people don't look to give others a word from God but God uses them often for that purpose. Of course you will always have your counterfeit prophets, just like you have your counterfeit pastors, teachers, and evangelists. Regardless, you must always ask the Lord for discernment.

Listen, if God has ever told you as a pastor that in such a time, your ministry would be thus and thus, you've received a prophecy. If someone told you the Lord showed them this or that about you and it came to pass, you received a prophecy. If God has ever sent someone to tell you as an evangelist to go speak in such a place because someone needed deliverance from whatever, you received a prophecy. Prophecy doesn't always have to do with something that was supposed to happen when Christ walked upon the earth, but something God has shown would come to pass or an instruction. Don't get locked up on man's interpretation of God. That was the problem with the chief priests, Pharisees, and Sadducees. They got to the point where they were so into self that they couldn't see or hear the word of God. Hebrews 13:8 says, "Jesus Christ the same yesterday, and to day, and forever." Jesus didn't change because of popular opinion or because someone didn't like what He had to say. God doesn't change, as He stated in Malachi 3:6, "For I am the Lord, I change not."

What is a prophet? They are simply individuals who speak the oracles of God. Prophets of the Old Testament didn't always speak doom and gloom. They did not always speak of things that would take place in the far distant future. Sometimes they just delivered a simple word from God. Remember when God sent Nathan the Prophet to give David a corrective word in II Samuel 12:1–12? That wasn't a futuristic prophecy. Remember the word God gave to Isaiah to deliver to Hezekiah when he was sick in II Kings 20:4–5? Again, it wasn't a far futuristic prophecy yet to take place hundreds or thousands of years to come. A prophet is a conduit for God's purpose. They speak something God has kept from man until that point or speak something God wants revealed at that time. They are in tune with God and can hear His voice when He speaks. Here's the kicker though, there is *no* prophet in the scripture that lived an obscured life when God spoke through them. *Zero!*

Truth: God's word shows that He gave apostles and prophets to the body for a purpose and time, and the fulfillment of that time is not complete. Therefore, yes, there are still apostles and prophets given to the church.

If you accept the complete word of God, then you will not reject the part you may not completely understand. Don't throw your opinion of scripture out as being fragmented or give solid scripture references to solidify what you're trying to establish. Rather, take your time to commune with God in order to get a solid direction of what He wants to be conveyed. God put these ministries in the body for a purpose. Therefore, it would be absolutely negligent to think that the only ministries left for the body were evangelists, pastors, or teachers. Note that the scripture denotes a pastor and teacher as one. Why? I'm glad you asked! A Pastor should also be apt to Teach. While their responsibility is to monitor the well-being of their flock, they are also supposed to educate their flock regarding their purposes in God. Now, you can be a Teacher, and not be a Pastor. However, there should never be a Pastor who is not also a Teacher!

The scripture even goes on to tell us why these ministries were given to the body in Ephesians 4:12. These all work together as one. They are as the body Paul talks about in 1 Corinthians 12:12–26. What God gave to the body would not be complete without all the parts He put in place. Therefore, a pastor cannot say that God only has need of them and not the rest, nor can an evangelist say God only has need of them and not the rest. I hope you get the picture because God's word is complete. Nothing should be taken from it or added to it. Because one ministry is not as visible as the other doesn't mean it doesn't exist or isn't important. They all serve their individual purpose as God has ordained them to be. Remember, Ephesians was written some sixty-four years or so after the resurrection of Christ. Therefore, its content will continue to be relevant and current until its appointed time.

All too often I hear pastors boast about having the most important ministry in the body when they are *only* one ministry in the body. You might say, "We're the heart of the body." Okay, without blood, you don't exist. You might say, "Christ is our blood." Correct! Without veins and arteries, you can't receive blood so you wouldn't exist. So you see, what Paul stated in 1 Corinthians 12:12–26 still stands true in every measure of the word. Those parts that seem less comely, we should bestow more honor. Some unwittingly get locked on Romans 10:14–15, which states, "and how shall they hear without a preacher? And how shall they preach, except they be sent?" In proclaiming the gospel, God can *send* a babe just recently converted to win his household, never having gone to church! When the scripture mentions "Preacher" in verse 14 it's not talking about a Pastor per say, but someone who's proclaiming the gospel, as it goes on to describe in vs 15 "…as it is written, how beautiful are the feet of them that preach the gospel of peace, and bring glad tidings of good things!" Therefore, the best part of the service is not the preaching, but the service as a whole. By the same token, the best part of the body is not the head, heart, or feet, but the complete body as orchestrated by God. Every part is equally important. Each part of the Godhead are equally important!

Ponder this. As long as the gospel has not been preached in all the world and there are still those who have not heard God's plan of salvation, then there will still be a need for a new church to be established. As long as God is still God, He will speak to and through whomever He pleases to establish a thing or give direction as He pleases! God is the same today, yesterday, and forever...an all-inclusive God!

Chapter 5

Jacob and Esau

We find throughout the centuries that man typically accepts whatever the popular belief is at that time. As a result, that belief is typically accepted without reservation. To that point, everything remotely related to that belief is developed on the premise of that foundational belief. This is good because without a foundation, any structure will crumble. However, if a concept, belief, or ideology is off a little, then the end result will not be accomplished or realized. A case and point would be NASA having their calculations off 0.0001 of a space craft exiting the earth's atmosphere destined for Saturn, and returning from that landing point back to earth. Chances are it would miss the earth by miles. A little leaven leaveneth the whole lump (Gal. 5:9).

Some might say a little fabrication here or there won't hurt, but it does. You may know the whole truth, but those listening or reading may not know the difference. Therefore, we must give exactly how God means it. If you want to give a different application, then make it relevant to the truth. Consistency breeds the same result *every* time. This is why God had the Levites trained on how to fulfill their ministry by doing the same thing at the same time, day in and day out. Routine. Now everything in life is not routine—and understandably so—but if God gives routine, He expects it to be followed. Where are you going with this? I'm glad you asked. If God gives you information in His word, then at least follow it. What God says should be enough, and absolutely nothing needs to be added to it in order to make it so. Now we know Hollywood always adds to a story in order to make it visibly acceptable. However, God's written word doesn't require that. God's word is good all by itself! Again, we can write and show the different ways to apply God's word, but the word itself needs no fluff. Otherwise, we run the risk of experiencing God's wrath as stated in Proverbs 30:5–6, "Every word of God is pure: he is a shield unto them that put their trust in him. Add thou not unto his words, lest he reprove thee, and thou be found a liar."

Doctrine: Jacob was a deceiver, and that's why
he was cursed to walk with a limp.

Now I've heard this preached a million different ways, but they all begin the same way—accusing Jacob of being a deceiver. Why? Lack of knowledge. I guess I understand how this account could be interpreted this way. We are taught by many a scholar to always read the verses before and after a passage in order to understand situation, time, and full account of what is being presented. However, many of these scholars fail to do the same. Someone came up with the idea that Jacob was a deceiver. For whatever reason, many jumped on the bandwagon and ran with the same belief. No matter where the information came from or the credibility of the individual delivering the information, we still have to validate their result. This is what Timothy meant when he stated, "rightly dividing the word of truth" (2 Tim. 2:15).

Let's look at the account of Jacob and Esau. We start in Genesis 25:21 where we see Isaac praying to God on behalf of his wife Rebekah, because she was without any children. As a result, God allowed Rebekah to conceive. Now, we'll notice in verse 22, that she didn't know what was going on within her, so she *prayed* to God for answers. God gives her an answer in verse 23, and she finds out she's carrying twins. Now I'm sure she was just tickled pink not having birthed any children, and then finding out she's carrying twins. At any rate, God tells her the fate of the two. She finds out that the *elder* would serve the *younger*. Now, she probably didn't even understand what that was all about. Now, we do know that his father Isaac was greater than his brother Ishmael; which was the younger over the elder as well. Now, the elder serving the younger is something we see throughout Israel's history, but that too could be considered doctrinal teaching. Therefore, we'll leave that alone for now. Now verses 24–26 tell us that Esau came out first, being the elder. We also see from reading further in verse 28 that Isaac loved Esau, and Rebekah loved Jacob. As we continue on reading verses 29–34 we find Jacob getting Esau to sell his birthright, and Esau agrees. Now we know that the selling of his birthright doesn't mean anything in God's eyes, because God knows who was born first; so a piece of paper means nothing. At any rate, we see Esau very upset because of this point. As we continue to Genesis 26:1–5, we see God confirming his covenant with Isaac, which was the covenant He made with Abraham. After this, we find Isaac negotiating with King Abimelech over some issues, and they eventually make a covenant together. After Isaac's issues with Abimelech are resolved, we find Esau rebelling against his parent's wishes in Genesis 26:34–35. In Genesis 27:1–2, Isaac was getting old and wanted to bless Esau, his eldest son, before he died. Now, verses 5–7 show us that Rebekah heard what Isaac had stated to Esau, and then she went to tell Jacob. Verse 8 is the major statement that holds the key to unlocking our understanding of how God works in terms of fulfilling His prophecy to Rebekah back in Genesis 25:23.

First Samuel 15:22–23 tells us, "Behold, to obey is better than sacrifice, and to hearken than the fat of rams. For rebellion is as the sin of witchcraft, and stubbornness is as iniquity and idolatry." One decree in the Ten Commandments says, "Honour thy father and thy mother, as the Lord thy God hath commanded thee" (Deut. 5:16). We even see in Deuteronomy 21:18–21 what was to happen to a disobedient child. Some even say these occurrences came after the Jacob and Esau incident. You're absolutely correct. Nevertheless, God is still the same today, yesterday, forever. Even before the Ten Commandments, it was their custom to obey their parents. I know that doesn't mean a lot in our society because we have extremely disobedient children in the church today. Much of this is due to families accepting society's version of discipline, not God's. Proverbs 19:18

tells us, "Chasten thy son while there is hope, and let not thy soul spare for his crying." It may be hard to hear but Proverbs 23:13–14 tells us, "Withhold not correction from the child: for if thou beatest him with the rod, he shall not die. Thou shalt beat him with the rod, and shalt deliver his soul from hell." Now this isn't condoning child abuse by no means, nevertheless, God has put things in place in order for us to maintain order in the family. Many have just put them aside because they really don't know any better. If they don't know any better, it's because they were never taught or never searched God's word to find an answer.

Moving on, we find that *Rebekah tells Jacob* what she wants him to do in Genesis 27:9–10. However, Jacob isn't comfortable with this command and explains himself to his mother in verses 11–12. Next comes the compelling statement from Rebekah on Jacob's behalf in verse 13. We see that Jacob views this act as *one of deception*, and doesn't want any part of it, because he doesn't want to receive a curse. Nevertheless, he is more concerned with being obedient. His mother tells him twice "obey my voice": once in her initial statement in verse 8, and then again in her 2nd command in verse 13. It's important to understand that obedience is *always* better than sacrifice. Now, we see how things were done in verses 14–29. We even see in verse 24 that Jacob lies in response to his father's question of who he was. *Why?* Because of his obedience to his mother's command. Is that okay? Many would say no because of our limited understanding in regards to God's plans and purposes. You see, God prophesied the end from the beginning to Rebekah.

One thing that is never mentioned—or maybe even realized— is that Esau was disobedient before the blessing was ever given. If you look back at Genesis 26:34–35, you notice this fact. Because God knows our end at our beginning, He knew the character He wanted before the boys were born, and He knew how things would work out in the transition of destiny. Much like Cain and Abel.

Now here's a thought. It appears that until Christ, the elder sibling took the back seat to the younger in terms of blessings. This may be a doctrinal concept, but it's food for thought none the less. From the time of Cain, the elder, it appears so. Cain was the elder of he and Abel. As a result of Cain's jealousy, he murdered his brother Abel, and was cursed forever. Now, of course time continues to expire, and we come to Abraham. Now, Abraham has two sons Ishmael and Isaac, and Isaac the younger is blessed above Ishmael. Then we see Jacob the younger blessed above Esau the elder. After this, we see Ephraim the younger blessed above Manasseh the elder. I'm sure we can find many other cases, but these are quick cases that come to mind. However, in the end we find Christ, the firstborn of many. Christ was the end of many things, and being blessed was one. No one will ever be as blessed as Christ. However, all can be blessed *through* Christ.

Truth: Jacob was never the deceiver, but the obedient example God predestined to be a father of many nations.

We see that Jacob was obedient to his parents, even at the age of around forty. At this age, many today would probably say to their parents, "Sorry, but that's not going to work." However, Jacob thought more of his parents. Let me take it a step further, and say that Christ did the same thing. We find in Philippians 2:8, "And being found in fashion as a man, he humbled himself, and became obedient unto death, even the death of the cross." Christ didn't have to do it, but He did. The Father told Him that was the way to redeem man back to Him, so Christ did. God doesn't bless or promote a mess. Jacob was destined from the womb to be a blessing to God's people. Therefore, whatever God allowed him to go through was for the benefit of His kingdom. God's plan was accomplished through Jacob exactly how God set it forth. Stop casting stones, and look at what God was doing. At the end of the day, ask yourself if God was pleased with Jacob. If your answer is no, then ask yourself why God allowed the blessing to come through Jacob. Some say that Jacob was just a deceiver. However, Proverbs 13:22 says, "the wealth of the sinner is laid up for the just." Hebrews 12:16 references Esau as a God-dishonoring person for selling his birthright. Just a thought.

By no means do I claim to have all the answers to the mis-doctrinal teachings of the Bible. Nor do I claim to have most of the answers. However, those things which God gives me to set straight, I'll be a ready pen. It has never been my intention to refute the doctrinal teachings I've heard over my years as a student of God's word, but for some reason God has given me this portion in time. We need to slow down, and go back to really spending time in God's word to be taught. If your doctrine has mostly been developed by what someone else has said or written, then take time now to reevaluate what you've been taught. Don't accept it at face value but search the scripture to see if it's so. I'm not talking about the history of customs, lineage, or even nationalities. I'm talking about the purpose, plan, and destiny of God's word. If you don't get anything, get this…there is only *one* interpretation of God's word, but *many* applications. Get the interpretation first then you can see your way to understand how to apply it. As long as you're spitting out truth, I can learn from it and add it to my library of information needed to minister effectively in order to grow the kingdom. It doesn't matter if you're older or younger than me. Good information is good information, any way you slice it. I'm not impressed with titles or positions. I'm impressed with the truth of God's word and the lives it changes. Selah.

Chapter 6

Angels

From our limited understanding of any existence, we understand that God has and will use anything He pleases to accomplish whatever He deems necessary to work out His perfect will. Therefore, if God chooses to use a drunk to minister salvation to someone lost in the streets, He'll do that! If God chooses to use a toddler to minister salvation and eternal security to an adult, He'll do that! If God chooses to use a woman who has been raped, abused, and discarded as nothing, in order to show His love and ability to forgive to someone who has a hardened heart, He can do that! If God chooses to use a newly converted teen to minister to a Pastor about longsuffering and obedience, He can do that! You see, God does not require that anyone or thing validate His actions in order to confirm that they are or are not good! When God speaks a thing, it is exactly what He has called it to be. Many times we want to put a natural twist on things we can't seem to understand, and God just says it is what it is! Many times when we don't understand a thing, we'll rush to put a name on it because we want to be the first to acknowledge its existence. What we should be doing is ask God for clarification so that whatever we do or say is decent and in order.

In this chapter, we are going to cover an issue that has always been a controversial topic in many denominations, and that is on the gender of angels.

Doctrine: Angels are males, as are Michael, Gabriel, and the ones who visited Abraham and Lot.

Now before the heaven and earth were created, we understand that the Angels existed. How and Why? Because there is no account of the creation of Angels, we understand that they were around before *"Time"* existed. Understand that "Time" only came into existence when God created the heaven and the earth. In other words, before earth, nothing had an expiration. Why? Because there was no sin. Angels are used by God for His service to bring a word from God or to perform a task for God. In some of the early scriptures, angels are seen being referred to as "sons of God." You'll find this as early as Genesis 6:2, 4. Then we see it again in Job 1:6, 2:1, and 38:7. The term *sons of God* is also used in the New Testament but refers to those who are in Christ. These references can be found in Romans 8:14,19 and 1 John 3:2.

Now, because of the nature God created us with, we always assume everything is formulated around our way of thinking. Because of this, we associate everything in life, regarding any being as having male or female genders. The only problem with this mind-set in spiritual things is that man fails to interject the feminine. What do I mean? I'm glad you asked. There is never an association made to a female angel. Man always wants to appear to be the dominant. As a result, we get a skewed viewpoint of reality. We associate Michael the Archangel as being male, because of his name. What if it were actually spelled Michal? Either spelling means "who is like God?" I gave you these 2 name references because one is associated with a male, and one with a female. We see Michael the Archangel as early as Daniel 10:13, 21. Then we see King Saul's daughter as Michal in 1 Samuel 14:49. By the same token, we see Noah as a male in Genesis 5:32 and as a female in Numbers 26:33. At any rate, angels are ministers of God sent to accomplish whatever task God has appointed them to do. They will appear in whatever form God has destined them to appear in. Remember, Hebrews 13:2 states, "for thereby some have entertained angels unawares." That could be in the form of a male or female.

Am I trying to confuse you? By no means! I'm trying to get you to now open up your understanding. Ask yourself this, what need has God with a male or female angel in Heaven? Male and female in our culture serve for companionship as well as procreation. It is not needed in heaven. Jesus states in Mark 12:24–25 (emphasis added), *"Do ye not therefore err, because ye know not the scriptures, neither the power of God? For when they shall rise from the dead, they neither marry, nor are given in marriage; but are as the angels which are in heaven."* We will not need companionship with each other because God is all we need. We won't look to honor each other because God deserves *all* the honor. There will be no need of procreation because God is the sustainer of life. Our desire won't be toward each other because God will be our total focus and desire.

The angels seen as male that appeared to Abraham appeared that way because of how we view things as humans. Because male is the dominant in most species on earth, we associate everything accordingly. As a result, there is no definitive evidence of angels being male. However, we do know there are no marriages in Heaven also according Matthews 22:30. The scripture says because there are no marriages in Heaven, we will be like the angels. Male and female works for the flesh, but when the flesh is gone, you won't know me as I am. I will be a spirit without the flesh and blood. This is also why Christ's disciples didn't recognize him after his resurrection because coming back, He put on a different suit of flesh. What's interesting about Christ's return and the fact they didn't recognize Him is that His flesh didn't see corruption, but yet He was not the same. For everyone else under the sun, Solomon said "All go unto one place; all are of the dust, and all turn to dust again" (Eccl. 3:20). Remember, when we are resurrected, it will be our spirit not our flesh. Being our spirit, I believe there will not be a distinction of male or female in the spirit.

Truth: There is no scriptural evidence that angels are either male or female.

Man has various viewpoints on the sexual orientation of angels. There are great paintings by renowned artists that would lead you to believe that angels have an alternative orientation while others displays angels in the masculine alpha. There are many views for many reasons, and they all have their own individual arguments. Some arguments are quite compelling; others lack substance. However, when considering male and female, first define the purpose of male and female. If it's not consistent in any given state, then it must be dismissed. Remember, God is the same today, yesterday, forever.

The one thing we must be very careful of is not putting God in the box as humans so often love to put Him in! We always try to equate God's actions, intentions, and creativity to that of humans. Ask yourself one question in regard to male and female. What was God's purpose of creating a male and female of every species? Why did He not create the female human before the other female species? The answers are really not that deep. However, they do require that you allow God to give you that revelation. You won't find the answers in some psychological manuscripts or in some lost manuscripts found after thousands of years. Some answers can only come from God because only God knows all things, especially those things that are directly associated with His creations. Some even teach that Lucifer and Gabriel were also archangels like Michael. Why would you teach this? There is nothing remotely close to backing this doctrine either. Unfortunately, it is erroneously taught. Search the scriptures!

Hopefully this has closed the door on those doctrines of angel's gender that continually circulate within the body of Christ. For those who have been entrusted with the ministry of being a shepherd over one of God's flocks, it is imperative that anything you are not able to definitively prove by scripture, you make sure you state that "it is of your opinion." Why? I'm glad you asked. You don't want to be a stumbling block for the babes in Christ or those not yet matured in God's word. Now we can think one way, but God can give us a true revelation to open our eyes. Nevertheless, when that happens, we *must* be mature enough to admit it to those we have mislead in order to keep them on track. To put everything in perspective, remember we humans associate everything with strength to the male gender. Why? I'm glad you asked. After God created man, He gave him the responsibility of maintaining His creation. Therefore, it is in our DNA to attribute everything regarding strength, protection, and security to the male gender.

It is understandable why many associate everything spiritual to many things in the natural. Nevertheless, that does not make all associations in this respect correct. While it is true that the natural man cannot understand spiritual things, it is also true that the spiritual man should not equate all things to the natural! The bottom line in this respect, is that if it's not stated in God's word, then it is just your opinion. True, some things should just be obvious when it comes to God's word, but many are just opinion. When it comes to the controversial issues that are not just spelled out, ask yourself, "What is the purpose?" Everything God has created serves a purpose. Many times when we don't really know or understand a thing. We'll just speak what we heard spoken or we'll just throw a thought out there. Not really caring how big of a stumbling block it may be. Let's be better and bigger than that and just state, "I'm really not sure." God's Word will back up any issue by His Word, if we just search it out.

Chapter 7

Rain

Isn't it funny how we can hear something that sounds good, and run with it as the gospel, even if we've never proven it to be so? People do it all the time. I guess it's primarily because people don't like researching as the Bereans.

Doctrine: It never rained on the earth until the days of Noah!

We find the first introduction of the word *"Rain"* in scripture in Genesis 2:5, which ties in to the complete thought beginning in Genesis 2:4. Note the explanation in verse 5 states, "Before it was in the earth, and...before it grew." Why? "for the Lord God had not caused it to rain upon the earth, and there was not a man to till the ground." We see there was a mist that watered the face of the earth, as covered in verse 6 of the same chapter. It's important to note here that this mist existed prior to God creating plants and herbs. God made the soil pliable first even before creating man! How do we know this? I'm glad you asked! Note that Genesis 2:4 starts, "These are the generations." It's very simple yet profound! This simply means these are the beginnings or this is how things transpired. It is also *very* important to recognize that verse 5 ends with three significant words, *before it grew.* Prior to this, we find six other significant words, *before it was in the earth.* Verse 6 begins with the conjunction *but.* This conjunction gives us the key to God's initial process of plant life. You see,

God prepared the ground to be conducive for what He was about to bring forth. Note that the mist came up *from* the earth to water the "*whole* face of the ground." This was not just the area of the Garden of Eden, but the whole earth! Why? I'm glad you asked. So the whole earth would be conducive to what God was about to do! You see, land without water or moisture is dead. There is no life in it. By the same token, man without God is dead. There is no life in him.

Stay with me now! Verse 5b states, "for the Lord God had not caused it to rain upon the earth, and there was not a man to till the ground." Listen to what is said here and how the conjunction *and* ties the two thoughts together. God had not yet caused it to rain because there was no one to till the ground. Now we know God doesn't need anything or anyone, but that's not what we're focusing on here. We need to focus on what is being stated; answer why it's being stated; and keep that thought as we move on! Our focus here is that first scripture states there is a genealogy to the creation of the earth and the heavens, the plants of the field, and the herbs of the field. Even so, God had not yet caused it to rain because there was no man to till the ground. Because of this, God caused a mist to water the whole earth. Now we see from verses 4–6 God has given us the end from the beginning! What do I mean? I'm glad you asked! In verse 4 God gives us the end result of what He did in process of creating the Heaven and Earth. Stay with me! Verse 4 states "These are the generations" or the genealogy (process) of the heavens and earth in the day God made them. Verse 5 continues, "And every plant of the field before it was in the earth, and every herb of the field before it grew." This is what it was because the Lord God had not cause it to rain yet because there was no man to cultivate the ground. Verse 6 follows nevertheless there was a mist in the meantime that came up from the earth that moistened the ground everywhere on earth. I know some of this is paraphrased, but as you read along you'll find it is consistent with the scripture. Now, this is just three verses we're reviewing, but they are very insightful. It is extremely imperative that you understand where we are at to this point in scripture because it is paramount to the foundation of this *truth*!

Now that God has created the seas, land, vegetation, and animal life, He creates man. God puts Adam in the garden and tells him to take care of it. God brings the animals to Adam and tells him to name them. God then makes Adam a helper, woman. In time, the *woman* was deceived (1 Tim. 2:24). At any rate, they were found guilty of sin by God. As a penalty for their conviction, God would now dispense their sentence. God gave the serpent his sentence first; then the woman her sentence; and finally Adam his sentence. Now Adam's sentence involved all other life on earth! However, for the sake of this topic, we're going to focus on plant life, and the ground. God told Adam in Genesis 3:17b "cursed is the ground for thy sake." At this point, things would not be the same with the ground/soil. Before, there was a mist that came up from the earth that watered the face of the ground. From here out, it would no longer be that way. Before this, everything was easy breezy in terms of cultivating. The ground was good for growing and reproducing after plant kind. However, now the ground was cursed, and things would now change. No more mist to help you out! How do you know that? I'm glad you asked! Stay with me. Genesis 3:17c states, "in sorrow shalt thou eat of it all the days of thy life." What does that mean? I'm glad you asked. It means man would now work hard all the days he lives on the earth in order to eat what the earth produces. He won't just eat what was planted, but he'll work hard to even get to what was planted. How so? I'm glad you asked! Genesis 3:18a states, "Thorns also and thistles shall it bring forth to thee." You won't just plant and reap, but you will work hard to reap! You will have to work to reap the benefits. It's important to note that at this point man was vegetarian. Man did not consume any type of meat until later. Anyway, God goes on to tell Adam in Genesis 3:18b "and thou shalt eat the herb of the field; At this point, we see that man's total nutrition comes from the ground. Then Genesis 3:19a states "In the sweat of thy face shalt thou eat bread, till thou return unto the ground." It would no longer be easy for man to exist on earth. After God dispenses His judgment, He then put Adam out of the Garden of Eden, "to till the ground from whence he was taken." Note that until this point Adam was not instructed to *till* the ground. It was stated back in Genesis 2:5b that "had not caused it to rain upon the earth, and there was not a man to till the ground." At the point of Genesis 2:5b there was no sin as of yet on the earth, so there was no reason for rain, and no reason for man to till the ground. We find that God gave Adam instruction in Genesis 2:15 "to dress it and to keep it." There was no hard work at that point. Adam did not sweat to dress and keep the Garden, because the ground was not cursed yet!

Now let's stop and think about agriculture today. Nothing has changed in theory since the Fall of Man. Without water, there is no plant life. *None!* All eatable plant life requires water. Do you agree? When there is no water on the ground, the earth dries out and no plant life can survive in it. Now, of course, if the mist continued upon the whole face of the earth after the fall, then Adam wouldn't sweat cultivating the ground. If we tap in to the wisdom God has given us and we ask the Holy Spirit for clarity of understanding, we would see and understand that God caused it to rain immediately following the expulsion from the Garden of Eden. There is no plant life without water, and there is no human life without plant life. Therefore, there must be rain in order for plant life to exist, which is also tied to the existence of mankind. Otherwise, there was nothing to sustain mankind. When I say immediately, I'm not saying the next second, hour, or day. I'm saying before the next harvest. Technically, we don't know what was going on outside the Garden of Eden. Scripture does not say. We do believe that every being on the earth did not reside in Eden though. Remember, prior to the Fall, and sometime after the Fall, everyone were vegetarian. I say this again because it's imperative to understand that man's and animal's sustenance was in plant life.

Truth: It rained hundreds of years before Noah came on the scene.

From our study of the scripture here, we understand that rain was not something new to Noah or those of his time. Why is that? I'm glad you asked. In order for mankind to exist, there had to be those who planted, those who cultivated, and those who harvested the crop. We also understand that God's sentence of judgment for Adam, which included the state of the earth, caused the ceasing of mist to water the earth. God would now cause it to rain, because He now had a man to till the ground. That's not saying that God couldn't cause it to rain, because He didn't have anyone to till His ground. That would be like saying God couldn't add more water to the earth, because it would overflow all the banks. If He wanted, God could let it rain, and never allow a plant to grow beyond its accepted height! God is all that, and much more. However, God allowed it to go this way for His purpose. God has a bigger purpose.

Hopefully, this brings better clarity to that Doctrine of Rain in Noah's day. If you've taught that initial doctrine, I pray God has opened your understanding to this truth. If you've never taught this doctrine, I pray God continues to enlighten you on rightly dividing His word.

Chapter 8

Women in the Pulpit and Pastoring

Within this movement we call Christianity, very often we find groups, ministries, suborganizations, cliques, etc., that like to set themselves apart from all others whom also call themselves Christians. By doing this, for whatever reason, they feel they are more spiritual and therefore are truly the only ones who hold the key to the mystery of God's love, mercy, and compassion. Some may think I'm talking about pastors, but you would be incorrect. This statement holds true for many parts of the body, be it evangelist, prophets, teachers, etc.

What is the problem with this way of thinking? I'm glad you ask! If I may from this point, let me associate these various parties with the common clarification in the body of Christ as "ministries." I don't believe I have to revisit what Paul said in 1 Corinthians 12:12–26 regarding the parts that make up the body. If you were able to grasp that concept, you will do fine with this chapter.

All throughout God's Word, the Holy Bible, we are given illustrations and stories to lead us to a truth. Jesus spoke many parables in order to accomplish the same result. The challenge for man is being able to properly understand, even though it's in plain sight to some. Nevertheless, this is why Jesus spoke in parables. The revelation wasn't given to everyone at the same time. To paraphrase what Jesus said in Matthew 13:13–17, the parables were for those who had religion but no relationship. Sometimes our religion stands in the way of God showing us what He's really trying to do. Basically, because our heart is not set in the right place to receive or comprehend what's going on. However, blessed are those who listen and see what God is doing. God knows the heart, and that has to be right before any critical revelation is given. As Christ quoted in Matthew 13:15, "lest at any time they should see with their eyes, and hear with their ears, and should understand with their heart, and should be converted, and I should heal them." In other words, if we would move from being self-righteous, which is sinful and diseased, God would renew our viewpoints and give us a better way of walking this journey called life.

Doctrine: Women were not called to be pastors and, thus, should not be allowed to speak from the pulpit.

There are several scriptures that are used to teach this doctrine that are totally misinterpreted and misaligned. One of the classics is 1 Corinthians 11:3, which speaks about the man being the head of the woman. However, if you don't consider the whole conversation, which includes verses 1–16, you'll miss the whole point of what Paul is really speaking about. It has nothing to do with the woman running the man or really even leading the man. It has to do with her veiling and covering. Now peep this! It does mention her praying and preaching! It mentions this in concert with the man's praying and preaching. However, it doesn't give man a special place to pray and preach from the woman though. It does state that neither of them are anything apart from each other in the Lord. You'll find that in 1 Corinthians 11:11. Verse 12 states "all things of God." Paul ends any disputations with verse 16, stating, "But if any man seem to be contentious", or if any man wants to argue the point, "we have no such custom, neither the churches of God." Paul and the early church had no problem with women preaching. It was only suggested that they do it with their head covered, even though it wasn't his custom.

Now, another passage of scripture misused in 1 Corinthians is 14:34–35 where it states that women are not to speak in the church at all but are to keep silence. As with our previous scripture, we have to read the whole scripture of subject to keep it in context. As you read 1 Corinthians 14:26–40, you'll find that Paul was discussing how things were to be done in order in service. We know from the study of 1 Corinthians that Paul was addressing a lot of carnal issues within the church. One of these issues were women just speaking out during service. Not just women, but everyone doing what they *thought* was okay. They were all trying to show who was more spiritual. That's why Paul stated in 1 Corinthians 14:26, "every one hath a psalm, hath a doctrine, hath a tongue." Everyone wants to chime in and take part. Have you ever been around someone who always has to have had the same experience someone else had? The difference is their experience was deeper or bigger! Those type of individuals always wants the attention to end with them and their experience. Anyway, in this passage of scripture Paul was addressing the disorganization of service at Corinth, and not women pastoring or preaching. Again, read before and after a statement in scripture to get the correct context and interpretation.

There are some who feel that a woman can't properly lead a man, and that is a sad way of thinking! There were many woman who had a positive contribution to our way of life today. If not for them, we would not be where we are today. Now some would say the same for men, and you are absolutely correct. However, we're not here to discuss men's contribution to the leading of our present lives. Let's look at a few women. We have Cleopatra who was the last Ptolemaic ruler of Egypt and lived from 69 BC to 30 AD. We also have Boudicca who led an army of a hundred thousand against the Roman occupation in First Century AD. What about Joan of Arc who led the French, and lived 1412–1431. How about Mary Wollstonecraft who was instrumental in extending human and political rights for women, and lived from 1759–1797. What about Harriet Beecher Stowe who was instrumental in the anti-slavery campaign and lived from 1811–1896? We are all familiar with Susan B. Anthony who also campaigned against slavery and promoted women's rights. There are many others we could touch on as well, but that's just scratching the surface.

All these pertained to things in the flesh. What about those associated with our spiritual state? We are all familiar with Mother

Teresa. She was our example of Christ's commandment to love. "By this shall all men know that ye are my disciples, if ye have love one to another" (Jn. 13:35). Remember, we lead by example. Stay with me now!

What do we say about Mary Magdalene? She was the first to experience the good news and the first to deliver the Good News. Why do think God chose a woman for that mission and not a man? Just something to think about and ponder till Christ returns.

Let's look at some other New Testament female leaders of scripture, starting with Tabitha, which is also called Dorcas. She is listed in scripture as a *Disciple*! She wasn't called a coworker for Christ or a follower of Christ, but a Disciple! We are typically taught that disciples were male students of Christ. However, this is the only passage of scripture that literally calls a female disciple by name (Acts 9:36–43). In Philippians 4:2–3 Paul, mentions two women as his coworkers in the ministry, and to keep on one accord in the Lord. They were obviously *Evangelist.* They were Euodia and Syntyche. In Romans 16:1, Paul mentions Phoebe as being a minister or deacon at the church in Cenchrea. It's understood that she functions as a *diákonos,* which is the Greek word that means "official servant." When it comes to *deacons* in scripture, she's the *only* one ever mentioned by named. In Romans 16:3, Paul mentions both Priscilla and Aquila as being his fellow workers in Christ. In Romans 16:3 Paul references this couple as Priscilla and Aquila, but in I Corinthians 16:19 he references them as Aquila and Pricilla. At any rate, they appear to be equal in ministry. Paul goes on to mention the church that was in their home in Romans 16:5a. If this church was in their home, and they were co-laborers, then that would translate *"Co-Pastors"*! Stay with me! Paul didn't see pastoring as being limited to men and helpers as women. Paul viewed us all as "one in Christ" (Gal. 3:28). Acts 21:8–9 tells us that the evangelist Philip had four daughters who prophesied (preached).

Let's look at a few Old Testament female leaders. We find in 2 Kings 22:13–14 that the priest, scribe, and servants went to inquire of the *prophetess* Huldah regarding the Lord's direction concerning the book they uncovered. She had to interpret God's plan for Israel's transgression of His Law. We see as far back as Exodus 15:20 God used women in the office of Prophetess. God has always used both male and female to accomplish His purposes! Miriam here is one of the first women of scripture to be referred to as Prophetess. Now we've covered Priscilla as a female leader of God's people in the New Testament. Now let's look at an Old Testament female figure as leader of God's people Israel. We will now view Deborah, who was a Judge *and* Prophetess. A Judge was an individual God *appointed* to lead Israel. The scripture tells us in Judges 2:18, "And when the Lord raised them up judges, then the Lord was with the judge, and delivered them out of the hand of their enemies all the days of the judge." We find in the fourth chapter of the book of Judges that Deborah was a prophetess who judged Israel, "And Deborah, a prophetess, the wife of Lapidoth, she judged Israel at that time" (Judg. 4:4). Read chapters 4 and 5 to get an understanding of who she was and what she did. It's important to note that the Bible specifically mentions that she was a *wife*, but that did not diminish who she was in God or the calling on her life. She was still subject to her husband and, obviously, submissive. Therefore, your calling and your place in the circle of life should not conflict with God's plan. You see, God ordains who He wants for service to promote His Kingdom. We should not get it twisted, and think that God *only* uses men to pastor His flock. How many men do you know that have been a stumbling block for the flock of the Kingdom. Remember, it's a heart thing, only extended by divine appointment! No gender, social status, or economic position specified! If God can use an ass to make a point, He is clear to use whatever means necessary to accomplish His will.

> *Truth: God gave various ministries to the church "For*
> *the perfecting of the saints, for the work of the ministry,*
> *for the edifying of the body of Christ" (Eph. 4:12), and*
> *those are to be filled with male or female workers.*

In the references we have stated in this chapter, the females covered every position of the fivefold ministry of the church. This includes our subject of female pastors. It's in the scripture. So those who initially thought otherwise should submit to God and accept what His word stated. Rightly dividing the word of truth is your focus and your ministry. You have been enlighten so stand on the truth!

Paul tells us in 1 Thessalonians 5:19–21 not to quench the Spirit and not despise prophesyings. We know that *prophesying* here is speaking about instructive preaching, as used in 1 Corinthians 14:1. Therefore, if you can learn and be edified from it, receive it! Paul then says in verse 21 of chapter 5 to prove it and hold fast to that which is good. Don't miss out on a blessing God has sent you, by holding the traditions of *man* and **not** God. Our nature seeks exclusivity, but God wants to dissolve that mind-set. It is very similar to the parable of the Pharisee and the Publican. When you think you have exclusive rights to God, you'll tend to alienate others without even knowing it. Even those who are currently in Christ can't alienate those who are without Christ because our job is to bring them into the fold.

Now having said all this, let's not worship the place a message is delivered from…meaning, the pulpit! It is the message that's sacred, not an item made with man's hands. I've heard many times "Don't touch that!" or "Don't stand there because it is holy and sacred." Not! Any place the gospel is taken is holy. Therefore, whether I preach from an old broken down milk crate on the corner of destitute lane or from the most elaborate pulpit in an elegant sanctuary, it is the message that saves and is sown. It is the message that's Holy, and not the place it's spoken from. Therefore, if a female is delivering a word from God, she should deliver it from the pulpit and not from a corner on the floor. Remove that haughty mind-set or God will! That "no women in the pulpit" is going to be the death of your ministry or it is the reason you have a dwarf ministry. At this point, given what you've just learned, there is no excuse. God is your judge!

Now I know many of you pastors and teachers can expound further on any of the areas covered in this chapter, which will probably be needed in many fellowships. My only purpose is to lay the foundation of biblical truth, not to pen a sermon. As usual, I pray God has given you what is necessary for your spiritual growth in this season.

Chapter 9

Life after Death and Recognition

When we are born into this world, something happens at the very moment we take our first breath. Our sinful nature is activated. This means everything with potential is jump-started. That first breath is the foundation for everything that follows. Our character is developed by our surroundings, associations, and any potential influences along the way.

One thing that is developed within most everyone that is born, is the desire for companionship. That is, the need to have someone around. Much of our development requires that we are nurtured through some form of interaction. These various forms of interaction aid in the development of our character. As our character develops, we acquire and acknowledge various familiarities in ourselves and others. Over time, we eventually accept these as constants in our lives and consider them part of our being. If these constants are missing, we don't quite seem complete. As a result, when a constant is removed, we often seek a replacement. If a replacement is not found, more than often that individual will continue to exist in an incomplete state. Also, many times this individual will end up in a depressed state of mind because of the feeling of incompleteness. Why are we like this? I'm glad you asked!

When God created man, He breathed into man the breath of life, and man *became* a living soul. Man was nothing, before God gave him life. Now, because God created man in the *likeness* and image of Himself, we should know and understand that man had intellect, wisdom, and knowledge. Regardless of how limited it was in comparison to God, God made him that way. With these attributes, man did understand he was *nothing* without God! Hence, his completeness was directly associated with God being a part of his life. When there is **ever** something missing in our lives that we were familiar with, we will *always* seek out a replacement in **most** cases! This, of course, is done in order to make ourselves *complete*!

> *Doctrine: We will see our loved ones and*
> *our pets when we get to heaven.*

I guess my first question is to those scholars who teach this doctrine as truth! Question is, who will inherit the kingdom of God? Shall flesh and blood? You can't straddle the fence with your answer. This question has a simple yes-or-no answer! Let's take a brief look at what the scripture says. In 1 Corinthians 15:47, Paul tells us that the first man was of the earth so he had earthly characteristics and the second man (Jesus) was of heaven so He had heavenly characteristics. He goes on to tell us that we are as our origin in verse 48 of the same chapter. He then goes on to tell us in verse 49 that even as we display the characteristics of the earth, we will also display the characteristics of heaven. Given this understanding, Paul then puts to bed any confusion in this matter in verse 50, "that flesh and blood cannot inherit the kingdom of God." We understand that an inheritance is something you receive. Therefore, the kingdom of God is not something that someone in an earthly body will receive because it's not earthly. Paul does not stop there, but he goes on to give clarity to that statement. He says that corruption (which is the flesh) does not inherit incorruption (heaven). Our bodies are aging every second, which means they are breaking down constantly until there is no sustainability left in them. This is just the nature of things on earth since the fall of man. However, heaven is a place of no aging or corruption so there is no deterioration or incorruption. Our bodies will be *changed* in the twinkling of an eye according to 1 Corinthians 15:51–52. What does that mean in the scheme of what we're discussing here?

I'm glad you asked! A change denotes something *different*, something *new*. You hear husbands and wives say all the time, "You've changed! I don't even know you anymore!" You also hear people say, "I know you like the back of my hand!" Truth be told, most people don't know what the back of their hand actually looks like. (See! You just took a glimpse of yours!) At best, we only know a very few things about people we are acquainted with and slightly more about those we are intimate with. Why is that? I'm glad you asked!

Because of sin, we are very reluctant to reveal our true selves to others. Therefore, others don't really ever get to know that person that is really easy going, and doesn't mind taking second place to allow someone else to feel good about themselves. You see, God and Adam had an open relationship like no other until sin entered the world. Adam conversed with God on a regular and had no reservations on how and when to approach God. However, after committing a sin, Adam found himself trying to hide and withhold things from God for no real reason. God already knows everything, but sin would have Adam think that maybe God doesn't know everything. Therefore, maybe I can withhold something from God. Not! Adam and Eve had an open free relationship, until sin entered! Now they find themselves trying to cover up their bodies. What before was totally acceptable without reservations, was now private and reserved. Since sin entered the scene, man has always been reluctant to reveal his true being. What we see now is only the outer housing of the true person within. Very few people really get to know someone intimately without reservations. People have been married over fifty years only to find out after one passes on that they were living a secret life. Again, this is the result that sin has played with man. You may love your child to death but you don't know the true person or potential that lies within. They will only ever reveal but a portion. Now there are those who are fortunate enough to learn more than average about one another, but those are few and far between.

Let's revisit 1 Corinthians 15 again. Verses 35 to 38 tells us that something must die before something is made alive. Also, that which dies does not look the same as that which is made alive. In other words, an apple seed which is sown does not look the same as the tree that grows from it. The same holds true of any seed that is sown. What also holds true is that *every* seed must die before it brings forth life. Even the seed of man must die before it brings about the conception of life within woman. Every seed goes from one physical appearance to another, even as stated here in these verses, "But some man will say, How are the dead raised up? and with what body do they come? Thou fool, that which thou sowest is not quickened, except it die: And that which thou sowest, thou sowest not that body that shall be, but bare grain, it may chance of wheat, or of some other grain: But God giveth it a body as it hath pleased him, and to every seed his own body" (1 Cor. 15:35–38). Paul goes on to state in verses 41 to 45 that we are initially sown with a corruptible body but are raised with an incorruptible body. The first body is sown of the earth (flesh) but is raised a spiritual body (spirit). The first is corruptible and the second incorruptible.

Our relationships are developed based on how we can satisfy one another. Therefore, all I know about you is based on how well you have satisfied me based on my needs. Whether I remember you or not will also be based on your ability to consistently meet my needs and desires. Sounds selfish, doesn't it? Well, ask yourself why you remember some people more than others, then you will come up with the same conclusion. Now there are always exceptions to the rule, but you should get the foundational understanding nonetheless. Marriage and friendships follow this same ideology as well. Keep in mind, this is all from an earthly point of view. From a spiritual point of view, we don't seek to be satisfied, but we seek to satisfy. We don't seek after each other, but God. When we are changed in the twinkling of an eye, our desire will be to please no one but God! There will be no other focus but God. This is why we read in Revelation about the four beasts, the four and twenty elders, and the many angels singing and declaring who and what Jesus is! There won't be a big social event going on, or people catching up on what was. We won't be catching up on how things were with our wives who left before we did. There are some who remarried anyway, had several spouses in the Lord, and passed on ahead. How would that look? Paul teaches in 1 Corinthians 7:32–33 how the married cares for the things of their spouse and how they can please them. However, the unmarried cares for the things of the Lord and how they can please Him. Because there will be no marriages in heaven, according to Matthew 22:30, our focus will be on pleasing God. There is no room to reminisce of the things done in the flesh where sin ruled most of the time.

This verse in Matthew also tells us we will be as the angels are. As we learned earlier, angels have no gender. There are some who would still dispute this point of knowing who you are from earth to heaven from 1 Corinthians 13:12, "but then shall I know even as also I am known." However, this is a gross misinterpretation of the scripture. This doesn't mean I will know you in heaven as I know you here on earth. First of all, when you are transformed to a spiritual being, the spirit that resided in that shell of a human will break forth. From a spiritual standpoint, at absolute best, all you know of a person spiritually is that they *may* love the Lord. That's even a hit or miss because you can't read the heart. Man's sinful arrogance would have him believe that he can read man as God does, and this is what makes him think he's not too far from being a "god.". Sad but true!

So what is Paul talking about? I'm glad you asked!

Well, we should know from reading this chapter that Paul is mainly talking about love or the sincerity of the heart. Paul begins this verse talking about not seeing through a dark glass, meaning we can't see anything clearly at this point. Nothing can really be made out. Then he says, "but then face to face," which means eventually open and clear without obscurities. We're still talking about love. We don't know what true love is yet, but we eventually will! He then says, "now I know in part," meaning he doesn't have all the facts or information at this point. Then he finishes with "but then shall I know even as also I am known," which means he will know and understand just as he is known clearly because God will open his understanding. Just as God clearly knows us, we will eventually know what love truly is. Too often scripture is used out of context to accommodate a point we are trying to make and may not even relate to what the scripture is actually addressing. Hopefully this passage is understood now and won't be used in context of this subject of "Life after Death."

Hopefully, at this point we understand that who we are now is much different from who we will be. There is a big difference between earthly and spiritual. Even after Jesus' resurrection, no one knew Him by sight. He always had to reveal who He was. Even walking on the road to Emmaus, they didn't know who He was until he blessed the food they were about to eat. They knew Him by His mannerism of prayer in the breaking of bread, but not from His prior physical appearance.

Truth: I will not know you or recognize you in heaven the way I know you on earth.

Now that we have a better understanding of familiarity with mankind after death, it should be easier to understand about animals after death. Though there are similarities between man and animal, there are also distinct differences. We both have skin, blood, eyes, and other characteristics of our physical makeup. We also both have a spirit. However, this is as far as it goes. Now, when it comes to life after death, there is no life after death for animals. Solomon makes it very plain when he says in Ecclesiastes 3:21, "Who knoweth the spirit of man that goeth upward, and the spirit of the beast that goeth downward to the earth." It doesn't get much clearer than that.

Truth: Animals don't go to heaven.

While we may establish many meaningful relationships here on earth during our lifetime, none of them will be carried into the afterlife. A lot of what we do here on earth moves us to cherish one another. However, in our life after earth, our focus will be on nothing and no one but God. All relationships here on earth puts God theoretically in second place. God deserves nothing less than first place! Now it should be understood we are talking about heaven, not what takes place in the New Jerusalem. That we won't be a part of. Anyway, that's a different subject all together.

I hope a complete understanding has been obtained from this study and a new perspective has been borne. Searching the scripture from the context that God is the total focus in heaven speaks volumes in understanding this concept.

Chapter 10

Fasting

Fasting or *to fast* are expressions used in more than just the Christian vernacular. For the most part, they imply the same thing. From a medical standpoint, it means to abstain from the consumption of food and/or liquids for a certain period of time. There could be many reasons, but they are all associated with the same intent; that is, to get you physically better. This could be in regard to surgery, tests, or whatever. It's a requirement for the preliminary to get you better.

Now from a Christian perspective, these are expressions that are fundamental to yielding a different intent—or I should say—a variety of different intents. Fasting from a worldly point of view is in alignment with attaining information on the body or in preparation with performing some procedure to the body. In either case, it's in direct association with the individual needing healing. However, from the Christian perspective, it's not always for the individual performing the fast. Christian's may fast for any event to take place, for an act to be perform, for spiritual enlightenment to take place, or even for a change in circumstances to occur. As you see, Christians can fast for many different things. From this perspective, fasting in the natural and fasting as a Christian both require abstaining from food and/or drink for some time. This is pretty much the definition given in the dictionary. One definition from the New World Dictionary of *fast* as, "to abstain from all or certain foods, as in observing a holy day."

Doctrine: Fasting is denying ourselves of food or drink in order to receive a blessing from the Lord or to do a service for the Lord.

There are several scriptures that cover the act of fasting. However, it seems Christians focus only on one aspect of fasting, and have thus created a half-truth of a complete doctrine. When you don't know a whole truth, you will only operate with partial knowledge, this cuts you short of the full benefit and blessing. It's like teaching money is the root of all evil People who operate on this half-truth will think that being wealthy is a sin. Well, the other half of that statement in 1 Timothy 6:10 says, "For the *love* of money is the root of all evil." When we have the full story or the complete information, we can make complete intelligent decisions.

A lot of times we operate on half-truths only out of ignorance. Paul mentions several times, "I would not have you ignorant" because he wanted to bring clarity to a topic or subject. A lot of our ignorance comes from not searching the scriptures ourselves. Every sermon or message you hear should be qualified by a follow-up from yourself. If you have not already read it before, then you need to search the scriptures yourself to see if what was preached was true. Not only will it increase your understanding, it will also increase your faith! It doesn't mean you don't believe what you've been told, but as a student of God's word, it is your obligation to search to confirm what you've received.

Let's look at a couple examples of fasting in scripture. First, let's look at the fast almost everyone is familiar with from the book of Esther, chapter 4. Now Esther *called* for a corporate fast to abstain from any food or drink for three days, night and day. Some fast for just the daytime and for after dusk. Esther's corporate fast was for **herself**. She wanted them to fast for her in order to have favor with the king because she wanted to see him outside of her appointed time, which was according to law. Otherwise, she could be killed. Esther wanted to intercede for her people so she needed favor to get through the door before she could present her case. Now, because everyone was in agreement, God gave her favor with the king, as you'll read in chapter 5 of the Book of Esther. So we see this fast was for self in order to accomplish a greater cause.

Now this next case is considered widely among many churches as a fast but really isn't according to scripture. Many have actually altered the structure of the content or items to accommodate their congregations. What case am I referring to? I'm glad you asked! The Daniel Fast. What occurred in the first chapter of Daniel actually was not a fast per se, but a devotion and commitment to remaining faithful to God. This all takes place in Chapter 1 in the book of Daniel. In verse 5, the king approved provision for all those considered worthy to stand before him for three years. At the end of the three years, the captives taken to Babylon should be ready. This would be their training period.

Now Daniel, knowing the paganism and idol worship that Babylon was known for, didn't want to chance defiling himself with the typical foods offered in the sacrificial worship. Therefore, he requested from the Prince of the Eunuchs that he would not be forced to defile himself, in verse 8, with the food given from the king. Now, the prince of the eunuchs was afraid of getting in trouble with the king so he was reluctant to honor Daniel's request. However, God gave Daniel favor, as told in verse 9. Now, we find in verse 10 that Melzar feared for his life in doing this because he thought that the king would notice that Daniel and the boys would lose weight and would appear malnourished. This would then be a neglect of duty on Melzar's part. Therefore, Daniel propositioned Melzar, the prince of the eunuchs, to give him and the three Hebrew boys ten days to prove themselves (verse 12). Daniel only wanted to be given beans and water. Some teach that this could have been a variety of vegetables and water. However, the scripture says "pulse," which would be a type of pottage that would be a mixture of peas, beans, and lentils or various plants having pods. Anyway, the key here is to initially be tried for ten days. Daniel wanted to be compared to the others who would eat the king's portion. Daniel told Melzar that after ten days, he could make the decision whether to let them continue with *pulse* or give them the king's portion. Read this in verses 13 and 14. We find that after ten days Melzar made the comparison and found Daniel and the Hebrew boys to look better. That's in verse 15. Now here's the clincher, in verse 16, we find that Melzar took away the king's portion for Daniel and the Hebrew boys and continue giving them pulse for the remainder of the three years. Now because of Daniel and the three Hebrew boys desire to remain undefiled, God blessed them with "knowledge and skill in all learning and wisdom." Not only this, but God gave Daniel more because he also "had understanding in all visions and dreams," you find this in verse 17. We find that at the end of the three years, there was no one found to be as gifted as Daniel and the three Hebrew boys. They were found to be ten times better than the rest. You'll find this in verses 18–20. The key points here are the **three years** training period, and the **ten day** test and trial period. After the ten-day trial period, they continued with that same diet up to the end of the three year period. As we see, this was not a fast, but a point to remain undefiled before God, which God honored in the end, and rewarded their dedication. You can say you want to conduct a fast that would model what Daniel did, but you can't label it a Daniel fast in good conscience. Many will call for a twenty-one-day Daniel fast and use this information in Chapter 1 to justify this corporate fast. However, I believe they're confused in mixing scripture. You see, in chapter 10, Daniel was shown a vision that troubled him greatly. As a result, he mourned three full weeks (Dan. 10:2). Therefore, he "ate no pleasant bread, neither came flesh nor wine in my mouth…till three whole weeks were fulfilled" (Dan. 10:3). This may also be considered a fast. I believe this where they come up with the twenty-one days. Take the time and read the chapter 10 in the book of Daniel.

Our third case is a fast never taught in our churches. That is not to say that no one has ever taught this, but of the percentage that may have ever touched it, that percentage is so low it would not even equate to a tenth of a percent. What in the world fast could that be? I'm glad you asked! This is the fast required of the Lord found in Isaiah 58:1–11. God told Israel they were really proud of themselves. They sought God daily and delighted in knowing God's ways. As a nation, they thought they were righteous and kept all the ordinances of God. They even took pride in being able to approach

God. However, God found them in transgression. Being prideful, they got bold and asked God if He didn't see the fact that they were fasting. However, God had to check them. In Isaiah 58:3, God told them that they find pleasure in their fast and decide not to do anything when they fast, which includes work. They were fasting to brag and to compare themselves with others according to Isaiah 58:4. God questions their method and intention in verse 5. God then asks at the end of verse 5 if they thought this was the fast He wanted. In verses 6–11, God lays out the fast that He has chosen, and the benefit that would result from His chosen fast. God lays out a series of things that involve the giving of self. He gives examples of various things that afflict the soul in different ways than just the abstinence of food or drink. He lists a variety of ways that involve abstaining from thinking of self. They all involve giving up self! To lose the bands of wickedness, turning from being deceitful in order to get gain. Undoing heavy burdens involves not requiring unnecessary work to get ahead. Letting the oppressed go free involves releasing those who don't have the help of others to pay a debt that is beyond their means. Breaking every yoke would be the same, not weighing someone down with unreasonable expectations. Dealing your bread to the hungry is obviously feeding the poor. Bringing poor in that are cast out is taking care of the homeless. God talks about clothing those who don't have proper clothing. He even tells them not to turn their own relatives away that are in need, at the end of verse 7.

If they/we adhere to these guidelines of God's fast, we'll receive the blessings that come along with God's fast as listed in verses 8–11. Our anointing/gift will be radiant, and our health will be sustainable. We won't have to brag on ourselves, because what we do for Christ will be obvious. God will *always* have our back. God will answer every prayer we request. Whenever we call on Him, He will be Johnny-on-the-spot. If we decide not to require more than necessary or speak ill of someone and decide to give of ourselves to the less fortunate, then we'll be able to make a positive impact on others. Those things that once burdened us will be lifted so we can see clearly; and the Lord will guide us in every way we should go! We will be satisfied with whatever situation we find ourselves in. God will give us that peace that passes all understanding! This is actually the fast that God requires of us—that we would give of ourselves. Is that really fasting? *I'm glad you asked! Yes!*

Even from the simplest form of fasting, it would be to abstain from something. God's fast would be to abstain from self. Don't think about being in your comfort zone. Don't think in terms of what you might get out of it. Don't think about being inconvenienced. Don't think about having extra for later. Don't think in terms of being put out. Don't think about what others may think. It's not about you, it's about others! It's not about your appearance but providing a comfortable appearance for others. If we can get to this place, we will be on our way to developing the character that is *truly* Christ-like! Christ did these things on a regular.

> *Truth: Fasting is not just the abstaining from food or drink for a period; but also the abstaining from self for a period.*

Come together and proclaim a corporate fast, but not abstaining from food or drink. Proclaim a God fast in whatever area or areas God leads you to focus on. It's not for vainglory or to be seen by men, but that God would receive the glory! There are many that are not able to take part in a corporate fast, but all can take part in some portion of the God fast. There is no reason not to fast in some form. The God fast is not for the benefit of the person fasting, but for the recipient of the fast. Remember, Christ coming to earth to give himself was not for His benefit, but for us, the recipients! We could never repay Christ for what He's done for us. In like manner, we should bless those who are unable to recompense the service. Christ covers this in Luke 14:12–14. We should give the full picture of fasting so no one feels left out, and all can receive the blessings from God.

I know there are other scripture references on fasting, but for the purpose of laying the foundation. The references used encompass those not mentioned.

Chapter 11

Tithing

This next subject of doctrine is one of very sensitive substance and quite often very misunderstood. Very seldom is this ever taught from the correct perspective that it was originally intended and with understandable reason. Again, that is not to say it is never taught correctly, but that it is seldom ever taught correctly.

Too often in the church, the message is watered down to appeal to the masses because no one wants to hurt feelings or offend anyone. There is also a lack of understanding on the part of the one delivering the message. This also could be due to a lack of study, research, or prayer. For the most part, it would appear to be a lack of prayer. I say this because God will *always* guide you in the right direction when you sincerely seek His guidance. However, if you are developing your message from something someone else has put together without researching for yourself as the Bereans in Acts 17:11, then you will miss the mark many times. I'm not saying you can't use someone else's research, but you still should verify their research. Remember 2 Timothy 2:15. Also and James 5:16, which says, "The effectual fervent prayer of a righteous man availeth much." James also stated, "Ye ask, and receive not, because ye ask amiss, that ye may consume it upon your lust" (Jas. 4:3). Therefore, don't seek understanding to share it in order to be praised for the revelation but to educate, encourage, and edify.

I'm not saying you can't be sensitive in your speech, but there is still a godly way to convey urgency without compromise. Colossians 4:6 says, "Let your speech be always with grace, seasoned with salt, that ye may know how ye ought to answer every man." Salt brings out the flavor of a thing. Salt also represents *strength*. Salt was required with *every* meat offering made to God. We find in Leviticus 2:13, "And every oblation of thy meat offering shalt thou season with salt; neither shalt thou suffer the salt of the covenant of thy God to be lacking from the meat offering: with all thine offerings thou shalt offer salt." Jesus said in Matthew 5:13, "Ye are the salt of the earth," which translates to "You are the strength of the earth!" Therefore, we can speak very firmly, and to the point; without trying to be politically correct. Remember, God is going before you to prepare for whomever your message is intended. Deliver it the way God wants it delivered without worrying whether or not you'll still be liked by the public.

Doctrine: If you want to be financially blessed, then you should be tithing. If you're struggling financially, it's because you're not tithing. The tithe is ten percent of your earnings.

Some of the questions we need to ask and resolve are:

1) What is the Tithe?
2) What was/ is the purpose of the Tithe?

Now, as I've alluded to before, I am not a scholar with three or four PhDs in theology or religious studies, nor have I travelled the world over to return with the answers to the meaning of life. However, what I do have is a heart to know truth from God's perspective and the Holy Spirit, which brings clarity to what has already been penned. It is from this standpoint of sharing what has been given to me so that we don't continue walking around in a fog and fail to "move on from milk!"

So, what is the Tithe according to scripture? The first time we see this term is in Genesis 14:20b. We find Abram giving a tithe to

Melchizedek King of Salem, the *priest* of the Most High God after Melchizedek blessed him. We don't see how much a tithe is, but only that it was a *portion* of all Abram had acquired. We don't find it mentioned again until after Israel is delivered from Egypt. We find it here as some of *everything*, whether of the seed of the land or fruit of the tree, is the Lord's and is holy unto the Lord (Lev. 27:30–34). Psalm 24:1 states, "The earth is the Lord's, and the fullness thereof; the world, and they that dwell therein." Everything belongs to God anyway. God is working a principal here that man is being conditioned for. Here in Leviticus 27:32 is where we find the second mention of a *tenth*, in terms of a tithe. Remember, Tithe is a *portion of all* that we receive. The first time a *tenth* is mentioned in this light is found in Genesis 28:22b where Jacob vows to the Lord "…and of all that thou shalt give me I will surely give the tenth unto thee." Now, stay with me! Jacob's vow to the Lord was to give back a tenth of *all* the Lord gave him. God's commandment to Israel was that of the tithe, which was a portion of all God would bless them with, a tenth of that would be holy unto the Lord (Lev. 27:32). The Tithe itself is a portion of all the Lord has blessed us with, and God has a purpose for ten percent, or a tenth, of that. You will see this much clearer as we move on.

We find in the book of Numbers that the Levites were the only tribe in Israel that wasn't numbered with the tribes of Israel, and not given an inheritance. We also find that they were tasked with the responsibility of the complete care of the tabernacle. This included setting it up, tearing it down, transporting it—and the whole nine yards. However, the Tithe was *their* inheritance. So to all it may appear the other tribes may have benefited; the Levites received the better portion. (Num. 3:11–12). Now, what does all that have to do with the Tithe? I'm glad you asked! God took the Levites from among their brethren to take care of the temple. As a result, they didn't have land, or livestock, to trade and make money from. So how did they support their families? God gave them a portion of the Tithes to support their families, while they were tending to the business of the Lord's house. We fine in Numbers 18:24 that of the Tithes of the children of Israel they were to offer a heave offering, and this was given to the Levites. Again, this was done because the Levites did not have an inheritance of land in Israel. The Lord then goes on to tell Moses in Numbers 18:25–26 to tell the Levites that of the *Tithes* which He has given them of the children of Israel of their inheritance, that they must offer a heave offering of that for the Lord, "even a tenth part of the tithe." So we see that a *tenth* of the tithe that is given to the Levites should be offered for the Levites as a heave offering unto the Lord. It goes on to state in Numbers 18:27 that this would be representative to the Levites as "corn of the threshing floor." In other words, this would be the best of their crops. Therefore, Israel would give a heave offering of the tithe, which is of their increase, and this went to the Levites. In turn, the Levites would give a tenth of this as a heave offering for themselves. This in turn, the tenth, went to Aaron and the Priests. (Num. 18:28). You see, according to Numbers 18:19–21, the heave offering was given to Aaron and his family because they didn't have an inheritance in Israel. God gave a tenth of all Israel as an inheritance to Levi according to Numbers 18:21 for their service in the tabernacle. We see that the Levites were chosen by God to tend to the tabernacle. Within the Levitical lineage, Aaron's line was called to be the Priests in the tabernacle. So for the purpose of understanding the order of things for worshipping God: you have Israel at the bottom foundation; then the Levites as grounds keepers of the tabernacle; and then Aaron and his descendants as the Priest of the Holy God. Therefore, Israel pays Tithes to the tabernacle, of which the Levites receive a tenth. Then, the Levites pay Tithes of ten percent or a tenth, of what they receive to Aaron and the Priests. (Num. 18:21–28).

As we research scripture here, we find that the tenth was not directly associated with the Tithe Israel was to bring of their increase; but was associated with what the Levites were to receive from the Tithe. The Tithe itself was to be the first fruits of all the Lord has blessed you with. We find in Nehemiah 12:44 that there were some appointed to receive and sort through what was to go to the priests and Levites that was from all that was offered by Israel. Hopefully, you've noticed that the Tithe was not a tenth of the increase from the masses, but a *portion* of what God has blessed you with. It is your first fruits; be it ten, twenty, thirty, forty, or fifty percent, higher or lower. Abram didn't give a tenth to Melchizedek, but "tithes of all" that he had received (Gen. 14:20). Remember, it was Jacob who vowed to give a tenth of all the Lord would bless him with (Gen. 28:22). This is not a pass to shortchange the Lord, but information to put us on point. Remember, 2 Corinthians 9:7 says, "Every man as he purposeth in his heart, so let him give; not grudgingly, or of necessity: for God loveth a cheerful giver". You know how you've been blessed, so your heart will have to tell you how to bless back. We also find in Deuteronomy 26:12–14 that every third year was considered the year of tithing. We find here that Israel was to gather all Tithe for that year, and was to give it to the Levites, strangers, fatherless, and widows. At this time, these groups were to receive from those who were the fortunate so that they too would have something during the year of tithing. This was the commandment of the Lord. God has always looked out for the less fortunate…and still does today.

So then, what was and is the purpose for the Tithe? I'm glad you asked! The purpose of the Tithe was to support God's work of ministering to His people. You see, in the Old Testament times it was to support those who maintained the tabernacle, and those who ministered to the Lord for the people. It really hasn't changed in these New Testament times. Tithes are used to maintain our place of gathering and to support the pastor and those leading the flock. The problem is the lack of understanding. If the shepherd doesn't really understand, then neither will their flock. The result will then lead the masses to what appears to be robbing God. Malachi 3:8 asks, "Will a man rob God?" It then tells us that he has robbed God in tithes and offerings. This results in curses for everyone. Malachi 3:10 tells us that if we turn around, and bring our tithes and offering, that God will bless us. Yes, but not because we're just bringing this. You don't get blessed just because you bring something, but because you're acting out of obedience. Many teach that if you tithe, you will be financially blessed. What about spiritually, physically, emotionally, or psychologically? You tithe because you want to, not because you want to benefit from it. Abram did not want anything in return. You should Tithe because it's coming from your heart, and not because you want to be in the line, or group, that's called upon in the church to be seen bringing the Tithe! Pastors, stop it! You don't make a separation in service that publicly displays those who are tithing, those who have an offering, and those who just have something to give. When Jesus mentioned the poor widow in Luke 21:2–3, she wasn't in a separate line or group, but she was considered to have given more than all who were casting in. Remember, God loves a cheerful giver, regardless the amount. God gave a commandment to support His ministry in Leviticus 27:30–34, and that has never changed; be it Old or New Testament.

You asked, where is it at in the New Testament? I'm glad you asked! Take a walk with me. Jesus gives a verbal reprimand to the scribes and Pharisees because they were focusing on the tithe and neglecting everything else in the law. Yes, we are under grace and not the law, but there are some principles God has carried over from the Law. These principals don't hinder our salvation, but they do yield a blessing none the less. Jesus says "these ought ye to have done, and not leave the other undone" (Lk. 11:42). In other words, the Tithe is important, but there is more than just the Tithe. Jesus knows, as we should, that the Tithes and Offerings sustains God's ministry here on earth. This is why God tells us in Malachi 3:10 to being the Tithe into the store house, so that there would be provision in His house. If there is not support in God's house for the shepherds, then God's word is not preached or taught effectively.

There was a time in Israel when there were not enough Levites to attend to God's work and Israel suffered. Because Israel failed to support the tabernacle, the Levites had to find work to support themselves. Because of that, God's word and presence was not felt. We find in Judges 17 the story of a Levite who was wandering around and looking for a place to sojourn because Israel had turned their back on God, and the tabernacle wasn't being taken care of.

The tabernacle/temple today is the church, not the Body of Christ, but the place of assembly. The priest/Levites of today are those of the fivefold ministry as well as those who take care of the place of assembly. This can be found listed in Ephesians 4:11–13. Jesus tells us in Luke 10:7 when He sent the seventy out that "the labourer is worthy of his hire." Having shared this, it should be evident that the church should be fully supporting the Pastor and church. Our Pastors should not have to hold a job to support their family. The Body should be tithing to the church and ten percent of that Tithe should go to support the Pastor. We see from scripture this is the case even today. Paul tells us in 1 Corinthians 9:13–14, "Do ye not know that they which minister about holy things live of the things of the temple? and they which wait at the altar are partakers with the altar? Even so hath the Lord ordained that they which preach the gospel should live of the gospel." It doesn't much clearer than that! So while there are those who thought this principle applied to Old Testament only, this is not the case. However, it is not properly taught how the Tithe and all this is to be applied today. Because the Tithe and money has been misapplied, any monies going to the Pastors is looked upon as corrupt. However, with the *correct* teaching of this principle, the body will know *what* to give and *why* they should give. They will understand that we are obligated to support the church. If our Pastors are living comfortable, then that is a direct testament that we are doing what God has commanded us to do, which is to pay a Tithe of our increase in order to *support* the ministry.

> *Truth: The Tithe of a tenth applies to the Priests and Levites, not the body. However, the Tithe itself applies to all!*

Now, remember that doesn't mean you can't give a tenth. We are required to give out of our increase, be it good or bad. If everyone were obedient to this command, then God's storehouse would be full to the over flow! This principle has been neglected throughout time more often than not. Even during Paul's ministry, we find him working outside of ministry. Paul took up housing with Aquila and Priscilla and worked with Aquila in the same craft (Acts 18:1–3). Paul had to support himself because the church had not agreed on what was required of them. However, today we have no excuse. We have the written word. We just need to walk in God's commandment concerning the Tithe.

Again, I know you Pastors can elaborate further on this topic, and I leave that to you. My only purpose is to open our understanding to this principal, and encourage you to rightly divide this truth to your congregations. Don't be afraid to express the fact that ten percent of all the Tithe brought in to the house belongs to you the priest/under shepherd. It's not because you're trying to get over on them, but because this is by God's design. No pastor or priest should have to work a secular job to support his family. God has given you this tenth so you could spend time receiving instruction from heaven and not worry about things that don't pertain to His work. If your mind is preoccupied with other things, you could miss some information meant for your congregation. Sadly enough, it's happening!

Trust God, and teach the correct purpose of the Tithe; and see how God blesses your ministry. Not just seeing how God blesses the ministry financially, but see how the people will be blessed. Don't allow the adversary to manipulate your ministry by keeping the people in darkness. Hosea 4:6 says, "My people are destroyed for lack of knowledge: because thou hast rejected knowledge, I will also reject thee, that thou shalt be no priest to me: seeing thou hast forgotten the Law of thy God, I will also forget thy children." Once this knowledge is shared and received, God's people can then act on a truth and God's storehouse can be filled. The result? God can open the windows of heaven. Blessings come in more than just the form of financial increase. Blessings also come in the form of healing to the body and emotions. Blessings come in the form of mended relationships, new jobs, houses, clothing, food, etc. God can bless in more ways than we can fathom. We just have to do what God requires of us in order to receive what He wants to give us when we obey Him. Trust God's word and see what happens.

Chapter 12

Worship and Praise

In the church today, there are many interpretations of what praise and worship is. None of them are really incorrect, but some are a bit misguided. There are many who view it as "their time to shine" and show what God has blessed them with. There are others who want to outdo all others and have the attitude, "Now this is how you do it." Then you have those who view it as the portion of service where people sing together before the preaching starts. Yet you have those who say, "It's not a real ministry." Even so, some go further to say it's not scriptural and should not be allowed in the church. There are even those who say no electrical instruments should be allowed in the church because that's of Satan. Then, of course, you have those who have been called to minister in that capacity.

Praise and Worship to some in the music ministry consist of two fast songs and then a slow song. For others, it may consist of an A and B selection before and after offering. In many churches, you have a music ministry where anyone can join and be a part of, whether you can actually sing, play, or not. Then you have others where you have to audition. In some churches, you have the leader of this ministry titled "minister of music." Even still, in others the leader may be titled the "choir director." Some churches have a group called the "Choir," and others have a group called the "praise team." Then you have some that have both. In some congregation you must be "born again" to be a part of this music ministry. While in others it doesn't matter. For some it doesn't matter what life style you're living; be it alternative, or otherwise. Some places just want a body, or talent.

Doctrine: As far as the music ministry of praise and worship in the church is concerned, God doesn't care if you can sing or play well, because God looks at the heart.

While this statement sounds good, it is not a fact. God does look at the heart of the worshipper, but that's not solely in light of the worship ministry. Meaning, having a heart to be in the music ministry isn't a license to be in it. By the same token, having a heart to minister God's spoken word doesn't give you a license to shepherd God's people. In both cases you're serving in God's temple; and in both cases you have to be called/appointed by God. I know there are other ministries in the body, but we'll look at these two for now. Regardless of the ministry in the body, they all share a basic pre-requuisite. You must be called/appointed by God. Anything outside of this is not God's will and is in jeopardy of missing God's blessings.

Let's look at this term *praise and worship*! So, what does it mean to *Praise* God? It means to acknowledge what God has *done* for you or for others. It goes even further to acknowledge what God is *doing now*! Through faith, you acknowledge what God will do in your future. This is your short definition for "praising God." So what does it mean to *worship* God? It means to acknowledge who God is! Here it's all about who, outside of what He can, or will do! In worship you acknowledge that God is glorious, marvelous, worthy, the *only true* God, etc! It's all about God's character. Too often we quote God's word, and act like we really understand what He's said. However, when it comes to ministry in the body, we act like Paul's breakdown of the body in 1 Corinthians 12:30 is a foreign language. There are some who get it, but for the most part many Pastors actually believe that their ministry is the most important part of ministry to the body. No so! Each ministry has its purpose to the body, and God's divine purpose would not be complete if one were missing.

So let's take a look at this music ministry. While there are tons of scriptures to support this subject, we will only cover a few. Remember, I'm only laying a foundational truth and not delivering a sermon. I leave that to those who are called in that capacity. We find Leah in Genesis 29:35 praising God after delivering her fourth child. We know from scripture that God opened her womb to bare children because she was the least between her and her sister Rachel. As a result of what God had *done* for her, Leah opened her mouth to *praise* God. Man has been praising God for a long time. In the old days, they praised God with more than just lip service. They praised God with their substance as well. We find in Leviticus 19:24, "But in the fourth year all the fruit thereof shall be holy to praise the Lord withal." When God brought Israel into the promise land, God told them to work the land in the first three years but not to eat the harvest thereof. However, after the fourth year, all the fruit was available to praise God with. Then in the fifth year, they could eat the fruit of their harvest. We see praise to God for what He has done for them, in giving them an increase for their labor.

As we continue to take a walk through scripture, we find a Prophetess and Judge named Deborah and a man named Barak, singing praises unto God for delivering them out of the hand of Sisera. You'll find their song in Judges 5:1–31. This was a song of praise for God's deliverance from an enemy. We find in Numbers 21:17–18, that Israel sang praises to God for giving them water to drink after a long journey. We find many songs of praise in scripture for many things. The common denominator is that God is *doing* something!

In 2 Samuel 22:1–51, we have a song of praise from David because God had delivered him from all his enemies, as well as from Saul. We know David to have written many songs of praise to God because he knew his source of protection. We know David was a skilled musician and played under the anointing of the Holy Spirit. We find in 1 Samuel 16:13–23 that after Saul had sinned, that the Priest Samuel anointed David, and the Spirit of the Lord was upon David. We also find here that David was a cunning player of the harp. He was known for his skill at playing the harp, as well as being known to have the presence of God on him. His playing was so anointed that he was hired to play for King Saul whenever he was vexed with an evil spirit. David's playing calmed Saul and removed the evil spirit (1 Sam. 16:23). After David was made king, we find David praising God with Israel on all manner of instruments in 2 Samuel 6:5 because the ark of the covenant was brought back to Zion. When David was celebrating, he was rebuked by his wife Michal. David did not care what she thought or anyone else for that matter. David was going to praise God no matter how he looked doing it (2 Sam. 6:20–22). Oh, that we would have that same mind-set when we entered what we term today our "praise and worship" service.

David had a heart to build the original temple, but God told him no, because of the blood he had shed. Before David's death, he gave his successor, Solomon, plans for how to build the temple. He also gave him plans for how things should be set up in the temple. This plan also included the divisions and duties of the Levites for service in the temple. There were many duties of ministry in the temple, but we are only focusing on the music ministry. You will find in 1 Chronicles 23:5 that while David was giving Solomon instructions for the service in the temple, he mentions that he made instruments for four thousand to praise God with. This should help those who don't believe musical instruments have a place in the worship experience.

As we study further, we find that David and the captains of the host broke this ministry of music down into three sections, which can be found in 1 Chronicles 25:1–8. You have the sons of Asaph responsible for interpreting God's word into lyrics. Then you have the sons of Jeduthun responsible for interpreting God's word on stringed instruments. Lastly, you have the sons and daughters of Heman responsible for interpreting God's word on wind instruments. These were all *skilled* in this ministry of song for the Lord (1 Chron. 25:7). This ministry was not limited to the temple only but was also used to encourage their army before battle, as found in 1 Chronicles 10:21. David is our best example of one who flowed in the area of praise and worship. David encourages us in Psalm 33:1–3 to praise the Lord with what we have and to sing to Him a new song.

David encourages us to keep our praise fresh and to play skillfully. When David and the captains made their appointments to this ministry, individuals were not selected because they just had a heart for praise and worship, but had no skill. No, they were all skilled in one area or another. They were not selected because they wanted to be a part of some ministry. No, they were appointed because they had skill. They weren't necessarily the best, but they all had a level of skill. There are those who have a heart but no skill, and they should remain a part of the congregation in this respect. They can still be a part of the worship experience but only from a corporate standpoint. Putting a person out of place in this ministry is much like allowing anyone to preach from your pulpit that has no skill, or calling, for that area of ministry. However, they have a heart to preach.

It's not hard to understand that when you have something out of place, the operation of a thing functions below the standard capacity of its purpose. Therefore, its original purpose is not achieved. There are many members to the body, and we don't all have to share the same function. We must all learn to stay in our lane so to speak, and don't aspire to have someone else's calling. We all have a purpose and calling. We need to seek God for what that is prayerfully. Let me rephrase that. Everyone in Christ has a purpose and destiny for a work in God. You must pray and seek God's guidance for where He wants you to be in His ministry. Then, step in and begin to fill your purpose.

In our experiences, we know we can praise God even when we feel defeated. David had to rethink his thought process and get a reality check when he was depressed in his soul. We find in Psalm 42:11 that David had to encourage himself to hope in God and still praise Him. Over and over again, we find David praising God for what He had done. We find Paul and Silas praising God in the midst of their trials as well in Acts 16:25. Psalm 139:14 shows us a praise for God because of His marvelous work. Psalm 145:9–10 shows us that God is good to all and that His tender mercies are over all His works. Furthermore, all His works will praise Him. Habakkuk 3:3 tells us that the earth is full of God's praise. Ephesians 1:6 tells us to praise God for the glory of His grace because He made us accepted in

Christ. We read in Luke 19:37 that the disciples praised God because of what they had seen God do. It may not be happening right now, but eventually everyone will praise God once the Lord uncovers all hidden secrets according to 1 Corinthians 4:5. The bottom line here is that like the Psalmist scribed in Psalm 136, we praise God because His mercy endures *forever*. We all have *big* reason for singing praises unto God!

We've covered a portion of what Praise is, and why we praise God. Now we want to move on to what and why we *worship* God. We learned earlier that we worship God because of *who* He is. Let's take a short walk, and review worship. Jesus tells us in John 4:23–24 that there would come a day, and it was now, that "true worshippers shall worship the Father in spirit and in truth." Jesus knew that there would be people who would worship from their most inner being, from the heart. He knew there would be those who appreciated God for *who* He is as much as because of *what* He can do. When we review scripture, we find in 2 Chronicles 7:1–3 that after Solomon made sacrifices to the Lord that the glory of the Lord filled the temple. We see also that the priests weren't able to enter the house of the Lord. As a result, the people bowed their faces to the ground and worship and praised the Lord saying "for he is good; for His mercy endureth for ever." (1 Chron. 16:34). To state "For He is good" is a form of worship, because it describes a characteristic of God (who)! When they state "for his mercy endureth for ever" also describes the characteristic of being *merciful*. This is directed from the standpoint of what God does for us in terms of dispensing mercy. This statement in 2 Chronicles 7:3 yields both *worship* and *praise*.

Have you ever notice how today we term our music ministry as "Praise and Worship;" with Praise being first, and Worship following second? In churches today we define a "Praise" song as up tempo, and a "Worship" song as typically a slower tempo. Thus, you have the term praise and worship. Even so, most churches will render 1–2 up tempo songs, before you get a slow to moderate tempo song. Don't get me wrong! There is absolutely nothing wrong with this. We recognize more often what God has done, than who God is! God has delivered us from so many situations, and has blessed us with so much, that we can go on and on about "what." Listen! How we present this to God will determine His reaction to our presentation. The first time we see this in a corporate setting we see God descending and His glory filling the temple. God's presence was so strong that the priest couldn't stand to minister. The Levites (singers and musicians) were all on one accord ministering unto the Lord. You will find this account in 2 Chronicles 5:11–14. We need to come together on one accord to evoke that same experience. Remember, Jesus said we must worship in spirit and in truth.

I don't know if you've ever experienced a service like this, but I have! I remember the Spirit of God had descended, and His anointing filled the sanctuary. It was so thick that my pastor didn't even bring a spoken word, because the word was flowing through the lyrics of the songs. God was pleased! You know your Pastor is not into self when they recognize that God wants to minister in a different way, and they allow Him! They don't quench what the Spirit is trying to do. Now of course, the Pastor has to be sensitive to the directing of the Holy Spirit. Key! Unity is the key with a pure heart. Remember what happened in the upper room when they were all in one accord? The Spirit descended upon them that were assembled together and gave them utterance.

God originally gave Israel a directive *not* to worship any other god in Exodus 34:14. We know other gods would include people, places, or things.

David wrote a song unto the Lord in appreciation of who He was and gave it to the worship leader Asaph, a lyricist. We find this song in 1 Chronicles 16:1–36. I want to focus on the lyrics in verse 29 that says, "Give unto the Lord the glory due unto His name: bring an offering and come before him: worship the Lord in the beauty of holiness" (1 Chron. 16:29). We know *holiness* is typically defined as "The quality or state of being holy". Of course then, this word "holiness" is taken from the root word *holy*. Though this root has several definitions, this specific correlation means "spiritually perfect or pure, untainted by evil or sin, sinless, or saintly." Our worship then should be pure and untainted by the troubles of this world! In the beauty of holiness! *"Hakuna Matata!"* No cares, no worries!

When we worship, we are to come in total adoration of God. The psalmist tells us in Psalm 95:6, "O come, let us worship and bow down: let us kneel before the Lord our maker." This means total submission of the heart, body, and soul.

In Zechariah 14:16–17, we find that those who set aside time to worship the Lord at the appointed time were blessed, but those who did not set aside time were not blessed. God wants us today to set aside time for worship. Way too often, we miss out on what God wants to do because we've failed to give Him His due! We get so caught up in trying to sustain ourselves or convince ourselves that we are all that, have already arrived, and that *true* worship isn't even on the radar. Either that or we are so consumed with troubles for tomorrow that we forget to worship the *only One* who holds our future. Sad but true! No one is exempt! We all fall short. However, we don't all have to fall completely out! We can all turn, and change our mind-set! We need to change our focus, and come like the wise men in Matthew 2:1–2. Christ had not done anything for them at this point, but they still came to worship Him. Not for what He had done, but because of *who* He was, they came to worship Him. This was not vain worship, but pure. Jesus talked about fake worshippers in Matthew 15:8–9. Those who present a form of true worship in appearance, but their heart is not for real. This is not in the beauty of holiness. Some teach doctrines that have no biblical foundation but is something someone thought up and put out there. Doctrine such as "Money cometh." This evokes vain worship. It's not from the heart, but from a place of self-gratification and accumulation. We should encourage others to worship God in spirit and truth. We can't worry about what others think, or say, because God honors the pure heart. Remember, Christ told Paul to step out there, and not to worry. They wanted to bring Paul up on charges for encouraging Jews to worship God contrary to man's law, as we find in Acts 18:9–13. Let's encourage one another to worship in spirit and truth without reservations!

In Revelation 4:10–11, we find the four and twenty elders worshipping the Lord because He alone is *worthy* to receive *glory* and *honor* and *power*! We also find in Revelation 15:4 that *only* the Lord is holy and that *all* nations will come and worship Him! We sing songs of worship that state God is so amazing; that He is marvelous, that He alone deserves our praise, that we will worship Him in the beauty of holiness, and many others. However, many times these are sung without any understanding of what is being stated. As a result, they are only songs in a group of selections. Many times the congregation doesn't even know or understand what's being said, either because the group ministering in song don't all know the words, it sounds confusing, or it's just new. At any rate, in this age of technology, we have these big screens that project words. If you are able to do this, then you have the ability to encourage the congregation to participate with an understanding. Imagine the change in your level of worship and praise that will take place. More of your congregations will be on one accord because they will sing with an understanding. Every fellowship has this ability in one capacity or other. It's about evoking a spirit of unity. Paul talks about the effect of unity and its ability to change the heart of the unlearned in 1 Corinthians 14:23–25. The term *unlearn* is not only limited to unbelievers but also believers as well.

There are some who think the praise and worship portion of service only prepares the heart to receive the spoken word. It does serve that purpose, but is not limited to that only. It does help create an atmosphere for God's presence, but it also provides a vehicle for the Holy Spirit to minister to an individual's need. When all participants are on one accord, you create an avenue for believers and unbelievers to unload their reservations, daily cares, and self-centeredness. There is no segregation of economic status or social prominence. We are all one worshipping and praising a holy God. You can't put God in a box. He is way too creative and uses what He will.

Truth: God does care about the skill set of those assigned to leading His people in worship, and He looks at the spiritual health of the heart.

Remember, we found in 1 Chronicles 25:7 that those assigned to this ministry were instructed and cunning. In other words, skilled. Why? I'm glad you asked! You must be able to solicit an atmosphere of unity. If you, as a group, are not able to create avenues conducive to the masses, then confusion sets in. This cannot be accomplished if you're singing or playing off-key or off-rhythm. There is a required skill set necessary at minimum.

Then there is the heart. Remember, Jesus spoke about the heart and vain worship in Matthew 15:8–9. If you are *harboring* sin in your heart that you have *no* intention of letting go of, you are not worthy. Therefore, this is not the ministry for those who choose to *hold on* to homosexuality, adultery, fornication, etc. It is what it is, no matter how talented. Satan was top dog, but it didn't matter to God. If these make up your worship ministry, you need to rethink your purpose as a pastor and make the tough decision to make it right. This is not about judging but getting to where God wants us. This is not about discrimination but keeping God's standard. If it doesn't line up with the word of God, then it is only man's doctrine. If we compromise this, then we hinder God's desire to fellowship in our midst. This ministry has a purpose, just like all other ministries in the body. However, if it's not properly staffed, its purpose will not be properly reached. All ministries are necessary in the body because each ministers to a specific group of individuals. Paul said in 1 Corinthians 9:22 that he became all things to all men that he might save some. Remember, one body with many members; and each have their purpose.

Now, I know we could go deeper and deeper into this subject, but as usual I'll leave that to the teachers and pastors. This was only to lay a foundational truth against some false doctrine. Everything has a beginning and purpose. The ultimate purpose of this ministry is to share who God is and to thank Him and acknowledge what He's done, is doing, and will do. This book of truths are just a few things God has given me to share. I've heard many pastors ask the congregation, "What are you going to do with what God has given you?" My father in the faith, Apostle LaFayette Scale, used to say the grave yard was a place of tremendous untapped potential; because in it there were books that were never written, songs never composed, buildings never designed, cures to diseases never documented, and the list goes on and on. I don't want to be one God gives something to, and never move in the direction He's leading me to accomplish a purpose.

I pray you've gained a working truth on something contained in this work. I also pray that you will take it and encourage someone else to walk in light of God's truth. Always remain a student of God's word and live 2 Timothy 2:15. I know I've addressed Pastors many times in this book, but it was not to pick on the Pastors. In your ministry it's important to rightly divide God's word, and it's important to give the proper direction to your flock. This was done to encourage you to walk worthy of your calling and trust that God has your back when addressing difficult subjects.

God Speed!

About the Author

I am the husband of a wife of sixteen years. We are a blended family with ten children ranging in ages from fifteen to forty-three. We have seven sons, three daughters, and eight grandchildren. I am from a family of seven. I gave my life to the Lord in March of 1984 while incarcerated. I've been serving the Lord ever since. The Lord called me while incarcerated, and He's been preparing me for my destiny using many avenues of learning.